N

Moors

40 Coast and Country Walks

The author and publisher have made every effort to ensure that the information in this publication is accurate, and accept no responsibility whatsoever for any loss, injury or inconvenience experienced by any person or persons whilst using this book.

published by
pocket mountains ltd
The Old Church, Annanside, Moffat,
Dumfries and Galloway DG10 9EB
www.pocketmountains.com

ISBN: 978-1-907025-51-8

A catalogue record for this book is available from the British Library

Printed in Poland

Introduction

The North York Moors National Park was designated in 1952, one of the earliest in the country. It stretches across a wedge of high ground between the North Sea and the Vales of Mowbray and Pickering, and includes the largest continuous area of heather moor in England. The plateau is dissected by tumbling becks and rivers flowing through wooded valleys. Ancient tracks stride along the tops, once used by monasteries and traders, now making ideal routes across the Moors, with wide-ranging vistas from the coast to the Pennines.

The North Sea coast makes a great arc around the Moors from Teesside to Scarborough, pierced halfway by the estuary of the Esk at Whitby. The cliffs rise to the highest point on England's eastern seaboard at Boulby, with a coastal path (the Cleveland Way) running the length of the Park.

To the west, the long escarpment of the Hambleton Hills draws the eye of travellers on the East Coast Main Line or the Great North Road, stretching north from Thirsk, with the turf-cut figure of the White Horse looking out from the hillside near the notorious hill climb of Sutton Bank. Further north, the curious eroded cone of Roseberry Topping gives a distinct profile to the skyline of the Moors.

In the south, a sequence of long valleys claw into the plateau, Ryedale, Bilsdale, Bransdale, Farndale and Rosedale all drawing water down from the wild uplands towards the Vale of Pickering. A series of attractive villages and market towns are strung along the base of the moors from Helmsley to Pickering.

To the east, great forests spread across the hills, offering miles of walking and cycling on forest tracks, with opportunities to link these routes to the higher moorland. Steep-sided 'griffs' or ravines have been carved into the landscape, notably around the Hole of Horcum and Newton Dale.

Across the middle of the National Park, the silvery Esk threads its way from west to east, countering the grain of the land which elsewhere has formed valleys from north to south. Most of the moorland settlements are spread along Eskdale, united not only by the river but also by the tracks of the Esk Valley Railway.

The Park Centres at Danby and Sutton Bank form the start points for a number of walks and provide information, exhibitions and resources. There is also a visitor centre in Dalby Forest, accessed by toll road.

The natural Moors

Away from the Park hotspots, you're unlikely to hear much other than the croak of grouse or the haunting cry of the curlew, echoing over endless open horizons. Forty sq km of the Moors are classified as a Site of Special Scientific Interest (SSSI) because of the distinctive heathland habitat found here, while more than one-fifth of the National Park is wooded. Much of this is accounted for by the coniferous plantations in Dalby and Cropton, but there is also extensive native woodland where you will find oak, ash, mountain ash, alder and birch trees supporting a range of birdlife. The long

Jurassic coastline offers expansive clifftop views, with hidden harbours and coves once the haunt of smugglers and now a magnet for geologists and fossil hunters. Because of the relative isolation of the area, there is little light pollution and this creates opportunities for clear stargazing. Dalby Observatory (in Dalby Forest) and Sutton Bank (on the western edge of the Park) have been given Dark Sky status.

Moors history

Although it is the natural environment that is the most enduring characteristic here, evidence of human history permeates every part of the Moors. Bronze Age burial mounds, dating back 3000 years, litter the open moor, while there are relics of Roman settlement, such as coastal signal stations, despite the remoteness of this outpost of Empire.

Whitby has its place in religious history as the site, in 664AD, of the decisive synod that determined the future direction of the church in Britain in favour of the customs of Rome. Arguably, medieval Christianity has had the biggest human impact on the scenery of the Moors, too. The remains of monasteries and abbeys such as Rievaulx, Byland and Whitby have become icons, while the legacy of their granges, or monastic farms, has shaped the present-day agricultural landscape. Many moorland tracks originate in the transport of animals and goods to and from these centres of Christian community, with a proliferation of waymarker crosses still standing sentinel on the high, lonely routes.

In the last few centuries, the stone and mineral wealth of the region has been systematically exploited. The large-scale extraction of ironstone in the North York Moors was central to the growth of the iron and steel industry in Teesside during the Industrial Revolution and contributed to the phenomenal expansion of Middlesbrough from a farming estate with just 25 residents in 1801 to 'Ironopolis' with a population of 90,000 less than a century later. There are fascinating remains of ironstone workings inland and alum production on the coast. Coal, jet and potash were also sources of wealth, some still extracted today. Flagged causeways were built to support this industrial activity, and these add to the network of footpaths and bridleways that explore the National Park. During the 20th century, extensive forestation took place in the southeastern area of the National Park, giving walkers and cyclists another very different environment to explore.

Walking the Moors

A number of long-distance trails cross the National Park, including the Cleveland Way, which travels 177km from Helmsley to Filey and takes in the entire coast from Sandsend; the famous 64km Lyke Wake Walk from Osmotherley to Ravenscar; the Tabular Hills Walk from Helmsley to Scarborough; and the Esk Valley Walk between Whitby and the source of the Esk. Aside from the official routes, there are miles and miles of trails, tracks and packhorse routes spanning the plateau. Some belong to monastic times, others –

such as the track of the Rosedale Railway – to the Industrial Revolution.

The 40 walks in this guide range from short and accessible strolls to full-day moorland and coastal expeditions. They are grouped into five areas: the Cleveland Coast, which comprises the northern half of the beautiful North Yorkshire & Cleveland Heritage Coast; the Cleveland Hills, including the country bordering Teesside; the Esk Valley, which runs through the heart of the Park, with all walks accessible from the Esk Valley Railway; Ryedale, Hambleton and the Southern Dales, focused on the valleys that meander south from the high moors; and North Riding Forest and the East Coast, weaving from the moorland plateau east of Cropton Forest, through the great forest of Dalby and down the Heritage Coast and beyond from Whitby to Scarborough.

The moorland plateau does not reach any great altitude, with its elevation peaking at just 454m at Urra Moor. But this is wild and remote country, and should not be under-estimated. There are long stretches of exposed wilderness; weather is fickle and walkers need to be prepared for upland conditions, with mist common and snow not a rarity; some access roads are steep and can become impassable in ice; and clifftops require obvious care! As with any walk, it is important to take appropriate clothing, footwear and provisions. The sketch maps in this guide will give you a clear outline of the route, but are designed to be used in conjunction with the two OS Explorer maps, OL26 and OL27, which cover every walk in the guide.

Public transport

Many walks can be accessed by public transport, which also makes linear trips more feasible. The main routes are:

Trains

- Esk Valley Railway: Middlesbrough to Whitby, calling at local stations in and around the Esk Valley
- Middlesbrough to Saltburn
- North Yorkshire Moors Railway: between Pickering, Grosmont and Whitby, with stations at Levisham, Newtondale and Goathland. As a heritage railway, out-of-season services are more limited

Buses

The following are key arteries with regular services, though varying in frequency:
X4 Middlesbrough-Saltburn-Loftus-Whitby
5 Middlesbrough-Guisborough-Loftus
X93 Middlesbrough-Guisborough-Whitby-Robin Hood's Bay-Scarborough
80/89 Northallerton-Osmotherley-Stokesley
128 Helmsley-Pickering-Scarborough
840 Coastliner Leeds-York-Malton-Pickering-Whitby

A network of buses also operate across the National Park on Sundays and Bank Holiday Mondays during summer. As well as key locations, these reach places that have no other bus services, so its worth checking the website (moorsbus.org) to find the latest services and timetables.

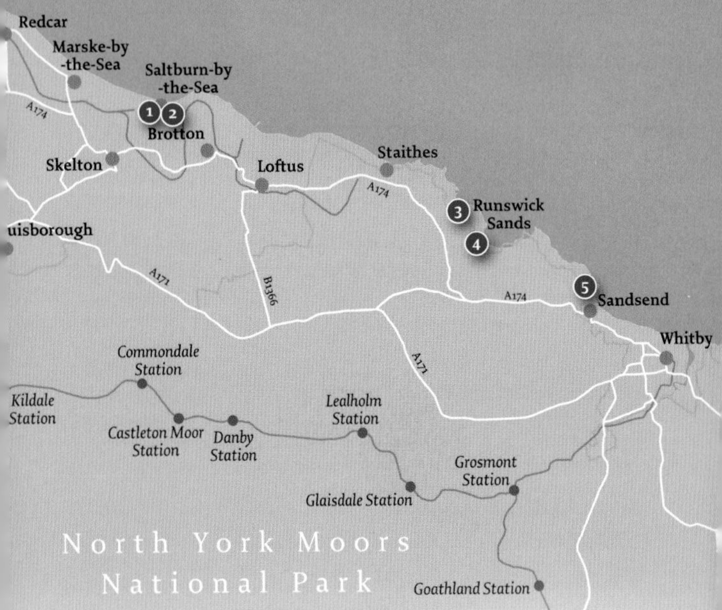

The Cleveland Coast stretches eastwards from Victorian Saltburn to historic Whitby, forming the northern part of the protected North Yorkshire & Cleveland Heritage Coast. The soaring cliffs rise to the highest point on the eastern seaboard of England at Boulby, just west of Staithes. Towering crags shelter hidden coves and sandy bays, once the haunt of smugglers and a stage for folklore, while the cliffs above Saltburn were the site of a fortified Roman signal station. The geology of this Jurassic coastline has been exploited for centuries, with shale, alum, ironstone and potash extracted from the rocks. Many industrial relics remain, while the area has an ongoing appeal for fossil-collectors and geologists. With the Cleveland Way extending the whole length from Saltburn to Whitby and beyond, this rugged north-facing coast now offers freedom and solitude for walkers, as well as an unspoilt sanctuary for birds and plantlife. This chapter explores the coves, cliffs and hinterland, beginning in Saltburn, a traditional seaside resort which is still popular today.

Saltburn beachfront ▸

The Cleveland Coast

Saltburn and the Valley Gardens

Distance 4km Time 1 hour
Terrain mostly surfaced park paths, some rougher sections Map OS Explorer OL 26
Access regular trains from Middlesbrough to Saltburn; local buses serve town centre

Saltburn is a Victorian clifftop resort, its working tramway connecting the town with the pier 35m below. There are many attractions here, making it a popular day out from Teesside. From the seafront, the Valley Gardens stretch inland through formal gardens to a wild ravine beyond. It's a short, easy walk, but there are one or two tricky and steep sections – so wear decent footwear. A tearoom is an added incentive, best saved for the return leg.

A road winds down from the town centre to the seafront and the settlement of Old Saltburn which predates the resort. In the late 18th century, smuggling was entrenched at every social level of this small community and, adjacent to the gin shops and inns, the deep wooded rift of the Valley Gardens would have offered a haven for contraband. There is a large car park (charge) at the bottom of the hill at the entrance to the gardens.

From the car park, cross the footbridge over Saltburn Gill, then follow the signs to the Italian Gardens and Woodland Centre, taking the left-hand side of Skelton Beck. The path flirts with the beck, crossing and re-crossing, until it arrives at the terminus of the miniature railway.

Cross the bridge and climb a few steps, turn left and follow the path up past the tearooms and education centre. A few metres after passing through the Woodland Centre gates (and shortly before a junction with the Cleveland Way),

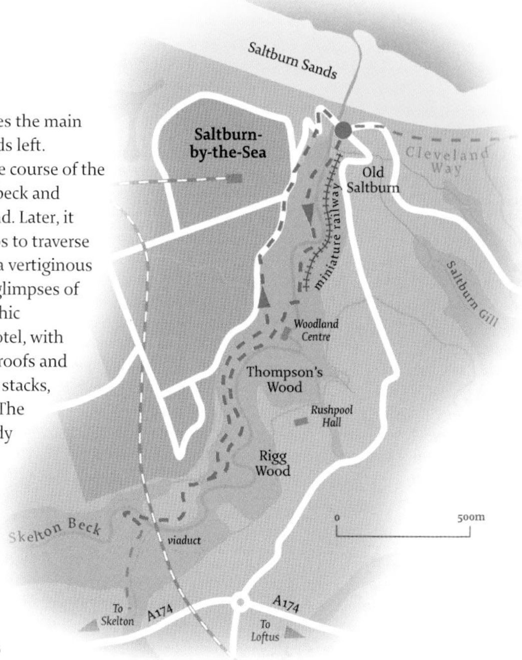

◂ On Saltburn Pier

a small path leaves the main track and descends left.

This follows the course of the valley above the beck and through woodland. Later, it climbs some steps to traverse the steep side of a vertiginous gorge. There are glimpses of the Victorian-Gothic Rushpool Hall Hotel, with its steep-pitched roofs and tall thin chimney stacks, across the abyss. The path can be muddy and the drop is steep, but the route is protected by a barrier and eventually it rises to meet a broad track.

Bear left here to accompany the track to the top of the hill and on to the end of the Valley Gardens. Turn left, now following the Cleveland Way downhill past Mill Field Meadow. At the bottom of the hill turn right, continuing on the Cleveland Way under the towering buttresses of Saltburn Railway Viaduct. Beyond the viaduct, carry on uphill for a good view of its impressive engineering and the dramatic chasm it crosses. (The Cleveland Way continues ahead to Skelton from here, a further 2km, if you fancy extending the walk.)

Retrace your steps from the viaduct and back up the hill to the entrance to Valley Gardens. Turn right, but then continue on the main track (the Cleveland Way) through oak and beech woodland, with an abundance of holly bushes. The track passes just above the Woodland Centre and then proceeds along Rose Walk, rising to meet a road above. The town of Saltburn lies ahead, ripe for exploration. Return to the car park by road or path.

Cliff walk to Skinningrove

Distance 6km Time 2 hours (one way) Terrain wide cliff path, undulating with steep climbs Map OS Explorer OL 26 Access trains from Middlesbrough to Saltburn; bus (X4) from Whitby and Middlesbrough to Saltburn; return by bus from Skinningrove to Saltburn

Wide sea views, dramatic cliffs and a rich diversity of wildlife offer a taster of the Cleveland Way, with plenty of history to unearth too. You can walk the coastal path in both directions or return by bus.

Begin at the car park (charge) at the entrance to Valley Gardens, where the road winds down from the town to cross Skelton Beck. Walk along the seafront towards the Ship Inn which is associated with much smuggling lore relating to the 'reign' of John Andrew, the village's 'King of Smugglers' and, in particular, Saltburn's legendary secret passages – which have sadly eluded all seekers.

Immediately behind the pub, turn left, leaving the road to climb a steep flight of steps. It's not such a long ascent to reach the clifftop and, once conquered, there are inspiring views ahead to the rock buttresses at Hunt Cliff. At your back lies the skyline of Victorian Saltburn, with majestic buildings crowning the cliffs above the town's lively pier.

Along the clifftops, a clear path climbs gradually towards Hunt Cliff. Wide arable fields stretch monotonously inland, contrasting with the dramatic seascape on the left. All the way to Skinningrove, the summertime path is bordered by ragwort, hawkweed, vetch, and, later, meadow cranesbill – attracting a fleet of butterflies.

As you draw near the whaleback of Warsett Hill, an information board marks the site of Huntcliff Roman Signal Station, one in a chain built to defend the area against seaborne invaders. Excavations in 1912 revealed the remains

◂ Skinningrove Jetty

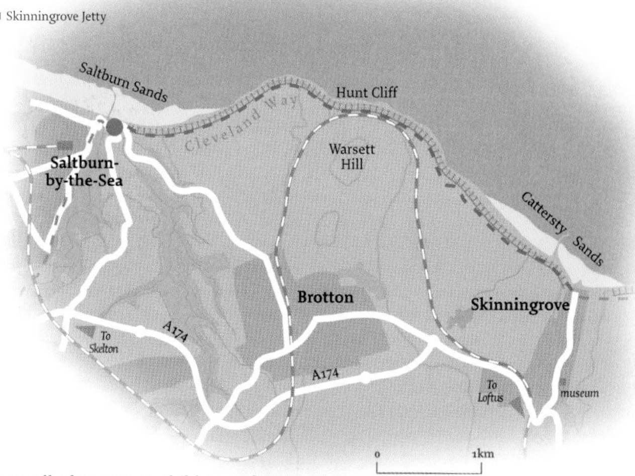

in a well of 14 women, children and men, most likely victims of a raid after the Roman garrison had abandoned the station. Coastal erosion has removed any traces of the site. More recent history is in evidence at the Guibal Fanhouse, built in 1892 to accommodate a massive fan (8m in diameter) which ventilated the ironstone mine operating below. Above the immense, shattered cliff, the path sidles up to a railway line curving around Warsett Hill. The line is only open for freight and continues as far as Boulby Mine. Originally it also carried passengers to Whitby and Scarborough on what must have been a world-class scenic line. Now a path and cycleway for much of its length, it clings to a narrow strip of land between the hill and sheer cliffs, with kittiwakes circling below in summer.

Just beyond Warsett Hill, a sculpture marks the summit of the walk. In the distance stands Boulby Cliff, the highest point on the east coast of England. After some open heath, the path turns left and drops sharply down steps towards the beach and jetty.

A track then leads beyond the jetty into Skinningrove. You'll find pubs and a chip shop here, along with a museum on the site of the former ironstone mine which once employed 500 men and boys; it's possible to explore the remains of its ventilation system.

Retrace your steps to the start or walk through the village to the A174. A regular bus service runs back along the main road to Saltburn or on to Whitby.

Staithes and the Dinosaur Coast

Distance 11km **Time** 4 hours
Terrain cliff, field and woodland paths; muddy sections **Map** OS Explorer OL 27
Access bus (X4) from Whitby and Middlesbrough to Runswick

Wander through fields and woodland to discover the picturesque harbour village of Staithes; then stomp back along a stunning stretch of the 'Dinosaur Coast', complete with fossils and mining relics.

Start from the crossroads at Runswick Bank Top, next to the Runswick Bay Hotel. There are a few roadside parking places nearby and a car park (charge) 300m on at the end of Bank Top Lane.

From the crossroads, follow Runswick Lane to reach Hinderwell where, about 1km from the start, you meet the A174 and turn right. In 100m, turn left along a public footpath between two buildings.

Follow the path across a housing estate, past a school and through a field, before turning right to take a green lane between hedgerows for about 500m. At a T-junction, turn left along an enclosed footpath, then head down through the next field and into a wood. Cross a footbridge at the bottom, climbing steps up the other side. At the top, go through a gate and keep straight ahead across a field. After a few paces, you'll see over the brow and you can aim for a gate on the opposite side.

This gives access to Oakridge Wood, where a pleasant but muddy path leads right and continues for about 1km. Soon after a sign for Oakridge Nature Reserve, the beechwoods give way to a lovely open glade with oak and birch, planted as an informal arboretum. Later, the route becomes a track and drops down, past a small caravan site, to a footbridge.

Cross the bridge and go straight ahead

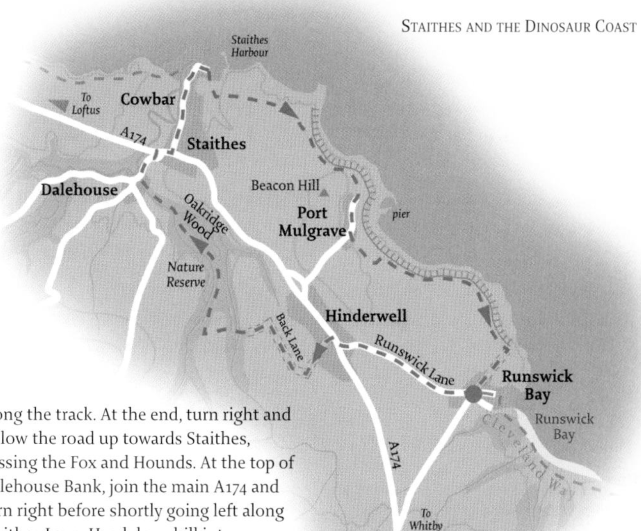

along the track. At the end, turn right and follow the road up towards Staithes, passing the Fox and Hounds. At the top of Dalehouse Bank, join the main A174 and turn right before shortly going left along Staithes Lane. Head downhill into Staithes village huddled at the bottom of a deep cleft in the cliff. This was once one of the North East's largest fishing ports, with a long association with the coble, a traditional locally-built boat. It must also have whetted the young James Cook's taste for the seas during his short-lived apprenticeship at the grocer's here in 1745. The Captain Cook & Staithes Heritage Centre tells more about the life of Britain's great 18th-century explorer.

Wind through the narrow streets to the harbour. Just past the Cod and Lobster, turn right and climb steeply up Church Street. Where the road ends, continue on the Cleveland Way beyond.

The top comes soon enough and the path continues on a clear line between fields. A short, sharp climb brings you right to the cliff edge, with far-reaching views. The path now traverses the top of the cliffs, later wheeling right to approach Port Mulgrave, once a busy harbour for shipping out ironstone and now better known for its fossils. Follow the small road past the first few houses. Approaching the main settlement, turn left, keeping to the Cleveland Way as it leaves the road and continues along the clifftop. The remains of the harbour and jetty lie far below. The path now runs between hedgerows before returning once again to the cliff edge. After a while, the wide sweep of Runswick Bay opens up, with the rocky headland of Kettleness in the distance. Nearing Runswick, turn inland past a pond (this once supplied water to the nearby ironworks) to reach the start.

◂ Staithes

Runswick Bay and Kettleness

Distance **8km** Time **3 hours**
Terrain **tidal beach (check tide times before you go), steep ascent, cliff path, railway bed** Map **OS Explorer OL 27**
Access **regular bus (X4) from Middlesbrough and Whitby to Runswick**

The coast path between Runswick and Kettleness takes in a beach, a rocky ascent and magnificent views on the clifftop finale. The return route maintains a more sedate gradient by making use of a permissive bridleway, looping inland on the course of the former coastal railway.

Start from the crossroads at Runswick Bank Top, next to the Runswick Bay Hotel. There are a few roadside parking places nearby and a car park (charge) 300m on at the end of Bank Top Lane.

From the Runswick Bay Hotel, go down the steep road signed for Runswick Bay Beach to reach a slipway (café nearby). Just to the right, a path leads above the slipway and onto the beach. Walk along the beach for about 1km, past the blue Runswick Bay Beach and Sailing Club. There is no way round this section, so you need to be aware of the tide, waiting if necessary. Soon after the club, the cliffline is interrupted by a rocky gully at Hob Hole, the caves here associated with the legend of a goblin able to cure whooping cough.

Turn right up the gully, using the shale side of a small beck. Soon, cross the beck and climb steps to the left. The ascent of the cliff is long and steep, but the gradient is steady and there is a good path all the way. At the top, a usefully-sited seat gives views back over Runswick Bay.

The broad grassy path continues along the clifftop, the red pantile rooftops of Kettleness drawing nearer with the headland of the same name spearing the waves. On the approach to Kettleness, the path turns inland, then loops around the seaward side of the farm buildings, giving a full view of the bare rock promontory below, scarred by extensive alum quarrying. Carry on along the road, through the hamlet, with the old station buildings and platforms on your right.

Shortly after passing the old station, turn right through a gateway onto a cindertrack. This permissive bridleway soon leads back to the line of the old railway which you follow for 4km. At first, it alternates between cuttings and embankments overlooking the sea. Later it swings inland, keeping to the higher ground and maintaining a mostly level gradient. The views diminish, though the surroundings are pleasant. The cindertrack ends by a red-brick house and yard. Keep straight ahead here. The route now follows a grassy course between trees for the last 500m or so. The path is obvious, but the last section may be a little overgrown before it drops down to join a road next to the site of a former roadbridge. Take care here, turning right and following the road for about 500m back to the Runswick Bay Hotel.

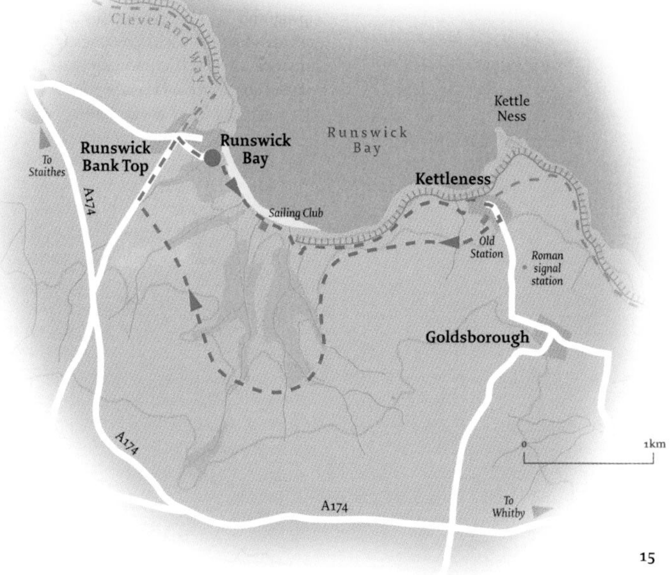

Sandsend to Kettleness

Distance 12km Time 4 hours Terrain Field and woodland paths and lanes, with one sequence of steep steps Map OS Explorer OL 27 Access regular bus (X4) from Whitby and Middlesbrough to Sandsend

The rocky bluff of Sandsend Ness heralds the start of the rugged Cleveland Coast stretching all the way back up to Saltburn. The geology of this seaboard has been exploited for rocks and minerals, evident in the quarrying above Sandsend and the alum extraction at Kettle Ness.

There is a car park (charge) at the western end of Sandsend, just at the foot of Lythe Bank, where the main road climbs out of the village. At the far end of the car park, steps climb the cliffside, signed for the Cleveland Way. These lead to a broad cindertrack, which follows the course of the old coastal railway between Middlesbrough and Whitby. The track contours along the steep cliffside, with fine views back to Whitby, passing through a jumble of disused quarries, now reclaimed by vegetation. An embankment carries the line between immense old workings and the sea; later a cutting separates the hillside from the rocky crags of Sandsend Ness. Soon after this, trains plunged into the darkness of the mile-long Sandsend tunnel. Today, the Cleveland Way bypasses this, climbing to the right of the tunnel entrance, using a sequence of steep and tricky flights of steps. These lead out of the chasm of Overdale and onto the clifftop.

A level grassy track now continues ahead, reaching a striking vantage point on the cliff edge at Tellgreen Hill. At a junction,

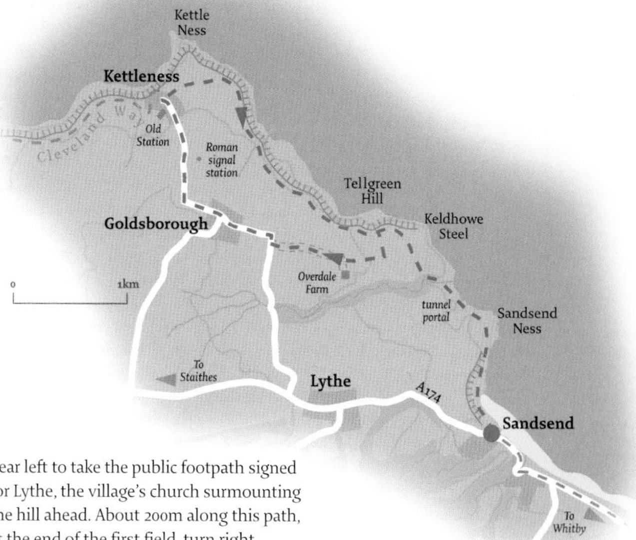

bear left to take the public footpath signed for Lythe, the village's church surmounting the hill ahead. About 200m along this path, at the end of the first field, turn right, following a track towards Overdale Farm. When level with the entrance to the farm buildings, carry straight on along the broad stony trail – aiming for Goldsborough on the crest of the hill ahead.

Turn right when you meet a road to enter the small hamlet of Goldsborough. Keep straight ahead at a junction to take the small lane signed for Kettleness. In a while, this bends to the right and drops down to Kettleness itself, with the whole East Cleveland coast opening up. It is not hard to see why this vicinity was chosen by 4th-century Romans as the site for one in a chain of signal stations dotted along the North Yorkshire coastline.

The old coastal railway crossed the road as it entered the village, with the former station evident on the left. Continue almost to the end of the road, next to a small parking area, and turn right, heading back along the Cleveland Way. The lunar scenery of Kettle Ness below is down to extensive alum quarrying. In about 1km, the path and coastline veer round in a more southerly direction, now heading for Whitby. In the breeding season, the alarm calls of gulls sound as they wheel above their cliff nests. The path climbs over the portal of the Kettleness Tunnel, though this can't be seen from here. It continues alongside a series of arable fields next to the cliff edge.

About 3km from Kettleness, at the Lythe signpost and path junction, you join the outward route. Retrace your steps to the start point.

◂ Sandsend

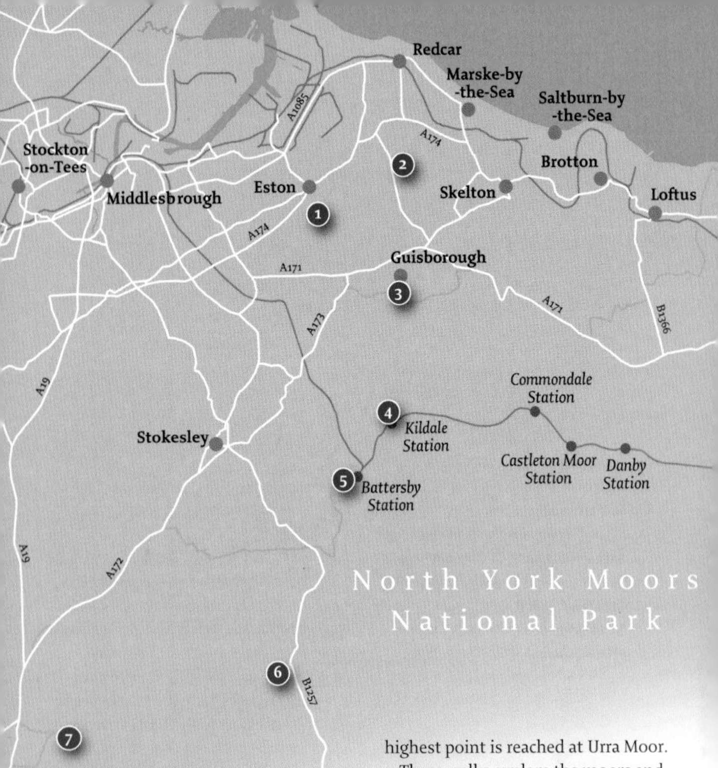

The Cleveland Hills curve around the northwestern segment of the North York Moors. They present a formidable profile when viewed from the Vale of Mowbray to the west or the agricultural land to the north. The distinctive cone of Roseberry Topping stands out as this area's most iconic landmark while, to the south, the highest point is reached at Urra Moor.

These walks explore the moors and valleys around the Cleveland Hills, including gems like pastoral Bilsdale. There are surprises just beyond the range, too, including the outlying hills at Errington and Eston Nab. Now sheathed by an altogether wilder natural beauty, there are still many reminders of this area's industrial past, from the ironstone railway that once crossed the moors to ancient packhorse routes that foreshadowed the Great North Road.

Iron Howe, Arnsgill ▸

The Cleveland Hills

On Eston Nab

Distance 6km Time 1 hour 30
Terrain tracks through woods and heath; some muddy sections and one climb
Map OS Explorer OL 26 Access regular bus (64A) from Middlesbrough to Normanby

Lowland heath is precious. The UK has one-fifth of the world's total, but it is rare in the North of England and Eston Moor is an important example of the terrain. This walk explores the moorland plateau – a patchwork of rough grassland with heather, broom and gorse intermingled with small areas of wetland. The wedge of higher ground rears straight from the coastal plain and so appears loftier than it really is. The summit at Eston Nab reaches just 242m, but its rocky edge commands a wide panorama across the Tees Estuary and up the Durham coast. It has been owned by the community since 2014.

A diagonal woodland path climbs the birchwood-clad slopes of Eston Moor to the plateau where there is an extensive network of paths and tracks. This walk uses wider and better drained routes, but there are plenty of alternatives and you can easily make up your own circuit.

Start at Flatts Lane Woodland Country Park on Flatts Lane, which links Normanby with the A171 between Middlesbrough and Guisborough. There is free parking and a small visitor centre here. From the centre building, walk diagonally up the field to find a small entrance onto the road in the top corner. Be careful here as there is a short, dangerous stretch of road. Turn right to walk beside the road, past Rose Cottage, for about 100m. Be alert as you cross the road to go through a gap with a footpath sign. A small path threads through the trees and joins a wider track. Turn left and follow the route through a gap in the fence. Quite soon, you leave the woodland and a wider path climbs diagonally up the hillside, which is dotted with gorse bushes and silver birch.

At the top of the hill, emerge onto the

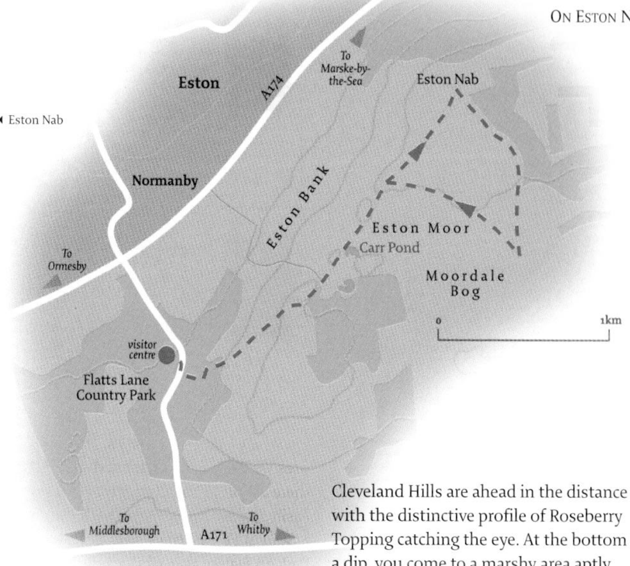

heath, an extensive area of birch scrub and gorse. Take the left option at a fork, aiming for the masts on top of Eston Nab. After a while, pass Carr Pond on the right. A good sandy path leads across the plateau, gently rising through grassland, heather and gorse to finally reach the summit.

The Nab is crowned by a stone beacon and a forest of masts, with a rocky bluff dropping steeply away to the Tees coastal plain. The beacon occupies the site of a lookout tower built during the Napoleonic Wars (around 1800). The Nab has also been home to a fortified Bronze Age camp and an Iron Age hillfort. At the top, turn right to follow a hardcore track gently down, with the biggest masts on the left. The Cleveland Hills are ahead in the distance with the distinctive profile of Roseberry Topping catching the eye. At the bottom of a dip, you come to a marshy area aptly known as Moordale Bog.

Turn sharp right here, almost doubling back. This track gradually climbs back up across the heath and through trees. In about 1km it comes to a junction with the outward route. Turn left and return past Carr Pond to the edge of the plateau, carrying on down the hill by the outward route. Remember to take the small path to the right, just before the bottom and soon after entering the woods. This returns you to the road and country park.

There are plenty of other walks through Flatts Lane Woodland Country Park. The area is a mixture of grassland and woods and was originally the site of an old brickworks. The Cleveland ironstone railway also passed through the site.

Errington Wood

Distance 6km **Time** 1 hour 30
Terrain woodland and field tracks with no serious ascents **Map** OS Explorer OL 26
Access regular bus (62) from Redcar and Middlesbrough to New Marske (1km from the start)

Errington Wood is a local nature reserve on the wooded northern flank of the hill between New Marske and Upleatham. This is a reasonably sedate outing with no big climbs but great views and plenty of industrial history.

Much of the woodland dates from at least the 18th century. Many more trees, particularly larch, were planted over the spoilheaps of the ironstone workings, which closed in 1923. At one time, these were among the most extensive in the country, fuelling the mighty furnaces of nearby 'Ironopolis' (Middlesbrough). Part of the walk follows the track of an industrial narrow gauge railway that linked the drift mines. Much further back in time, there is evidence of Bronze Age burial mounds on the top of the hill. Today, the woods are a peaceful haven for trees, flowers and wildlife, enjoyed through an extensive network of paths.

The walk encircles the hill, first through woodland, then returning through fields and the village of Upleatham. There is an ample car park and picnic area just off Sandy Lane, 1km south of New Marske.

At the far end of the car park, go through the gate near the information board. This leads onto a woodland track, the course of the original narrow gauge railway linking the ironstone workings. In the cutting, pass some wooden sculptures, including an owl and then a heron close to a small pool.

Keep straight ahead at a lane crossing. The trees thin out with pleasant mixed woodland allowing open views across the nearby coast and the Tees Estuary. In

◂ Errington Wood

another 1km, arrive at a T-junction. Turn right up the bridleway, ignoring any side turnings to soon emerge from the trees at the top of a short climb.

The path continues ahead, now contouring around grass slopes, with views eastwards towards Skelton. As it approaches Upleatham, the path becomes a green lane and enters the village.

Continue straight ahead through the main street of this tranquil and well-heeled township. At the far end, leave the road as it turns left, instead keeping straight ahead onto a lane and bridleway towards Errington Wood.

When the lane turns right into a farm, continue ahead to accompany the bridleway up the next field. At the top, pass through a gate and turn left at the junction of tracks. Soon this track ends at a gate. Beyond this, follow the path down the next field to a gate in the bottom corner. This leads to a green lane, Sandy Lane, which weaves around the side of the hill between woods and fields, with holly trees much in evidence.

In 1km, at a crossing of paths, carry straight on. The car park is soon visible down in front. There are various shortcuts, thought the easiest way is to continue along the path and double back along the main track in a few hundred metres.

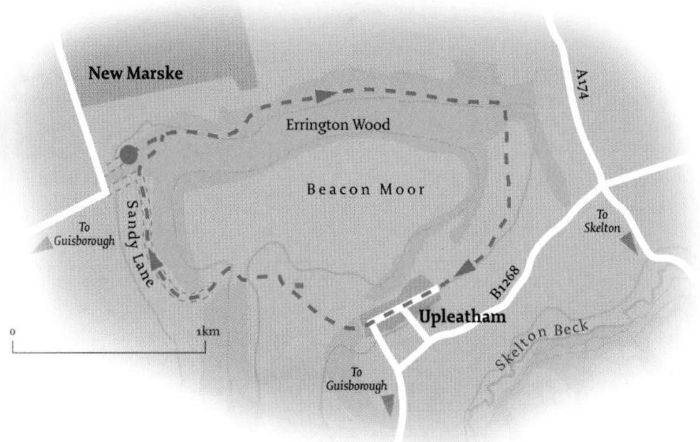

Roseberry Topping by the Cleveland Way

Distance **7km** Time **2 hours**
Terrain **woodland and moorland tracks with an easy clamber up the rocky summit** Map **OS Explorer OL 26**
Access **bus (5/5A) from Middlesbrough to the main road through Guisborough (1km from the start)**

Size isn't everything. Although only 320m (just over 1000 feet) high, the totemic Roseberry Topping punches well above its altitude – offering the aura of a mountain without a long, lung-wrenching ascent. The well-graded forest track to the top is followed by a taste of moorland along the escarpment, with the final rocky pyramid gained without difficulty. The reward is an airy panorama looking across a broad expanse of Northern England.

Hutton Village is hidden away in a cleft in the wooded northern escarpment of the Cleveland Hills, just south of the historic town of Guisborough; access is by Hutton Village Road, a cul-de-sac ending at the village. Drivers can park on the roadside before the 'Hutton Village' sign.

Just after this sign, bear right up a track signposted for Kildale and Commondale, which climbs steadily through the woods with glimpses down through the trees to the village. Keep straight ahead, ignoring side turnings and the cycleway crossing the track further up. At the top of the woodland, after a felled area, you come to a junction of tracks.

This is the Cleveland Way, a 177km-long national trail circumnavigating the North York Moors from Helmsley to Filey and

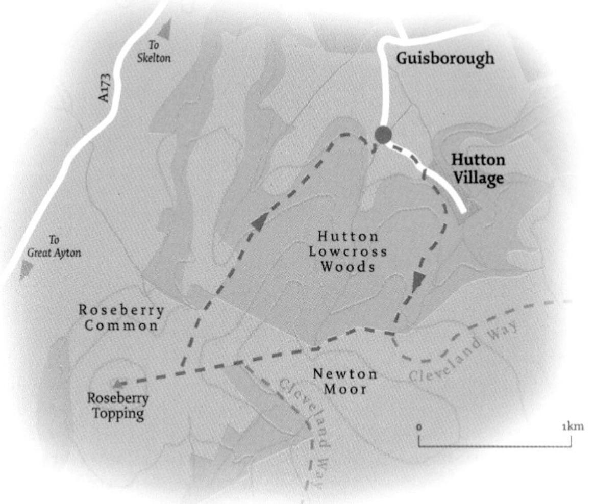

grazing the edge of the escarpment above Guisborough. Turn right to follow the Way, past a barrier and along the edge of the heather moor. In about 750m, bear left through a gate, staying with the Cleveland Way as it climbs and then dips to a path junction by a wood and a wall.

Continue ahead, passing through the gate and following the stone track down the hill with Roseberry Topping looming before you. At the bottom, cross the depression to a path junction and take the route that zigzags up to the summit. The steep but short climb is rewarded by magnificent views from this iconic rocky outpost of the North York Moors. It is likely that a young James Cook enjoyed this very view, his family having moved to Aireyholme Farm on the southern slopes of Roseberry Topping when he was a small boy. While working as a farm-hand for his father in 1741, he made frequent expeditions to the summit which, it is said, gave him the appetite for adventure that drove him to become one of Britain's most celebrated explorers. However, Cook's 18th-century Roseberry Topping would have looked very different from that seen today. In 1912, a geological fault, exacerbated by unstable mine workings, led to the partial collapse of the hill, creating its distinct profile.

From the summit, return down the zigzag path to the depression, turning left at the path junction. A wide path drifts gently down across the bracken-clad saddle, soon arriving at a gate into woodland. Here, a broad track makes a gradual descent back through Hutton Lowcross Woods to the road and start.

◂ Roseberry Topping

The Captain Cook Round

Distance 13km **Time** 3 hours 30
Terrain quiet lanes and good tracks, muddy at times; one easy but steep scramble **Map** OS Explorer OL 26
Access train to Kildale Station on the Middlesbrough to Whitby (Esk Valley) Line (around four trains daily)

The dramatic profile of Roseberry Topping pierces the skyline for many miles. Despite its modest 320m height, its Matterhorn-like summit is one of two great landmarks on the Cleveland escarpment. The other is the 16m-high monument to local boy, Captain James Cook. Both sites offer expansive views on this grand tour of moor and wood on the very edge of the National Park.

Start from Kildale Station, where there is also a small car park and toilets. Follow the station approach road back to the village. About 25m before reaching the 'main' road, turn left to follow the lane signposted for the Cleveland Way. Pass under the railway and across the infant River Leven, a tributary of the Tees.

Climb steadily with the parish church in sight across fields to the left. Although the present building is Victorian, the site has been home to a church and castle since Saxon times. Continue along the quiet lane as it winds up past Bankside Farm and over the hill at Pale End Plantation with beech, larch and oak trees shading the road. It descends into a small valley, crossing Lonsdale Beck. Leave the lane where it turns sharp left by some farm buildings and continue straight ahead through a gate and onto a signed track leading up the side of Nab End Wood.

This weaves up to open moorland and a junction at the end of a tarmac lane. Bear left through a gate and then keep straight ahead on the main track (also a cycleway) across the moor. After just over 1km, the Cleveland Way sidles in from the right; soon afterwards, go through a gate to meet a junction of tracks. Stick with the

◂ Captain Cook's Monument

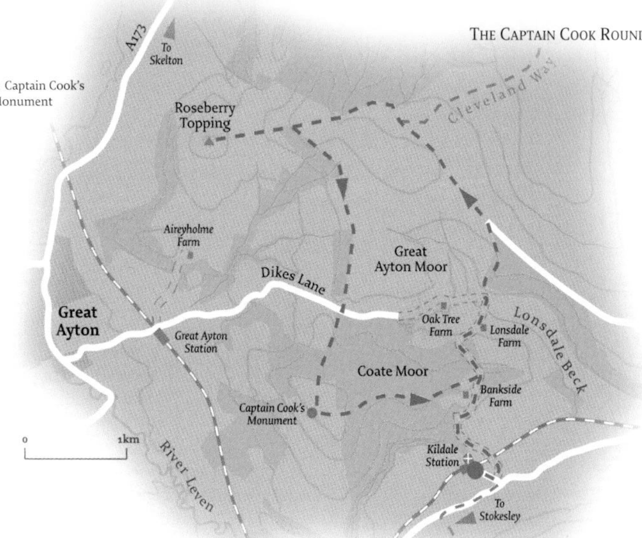

Cleveland Way by turning left and, after 750m, bearing left again through a gate. The Way climbs and then drops slightly to a junction of paths by a wood and a wall.

Carry straight on through a gate and down a stone track with the cone of Roseberry Topping looming before you. At the bottom, cross the depression and climb the zigzag path to the summit. Although this eastern flank is impressive, the route is clear and easy. The distinctive top dominates the landscape for miles around.

Retrace your steps for 1km, then turn right after the wall to stay with the Cleveland Way, signed for Kildale. Continue across the edge of Great Ayton Moor for 2km before dropping to a tarmac lane and moorland car park at Gribdale.

Cross the road and go through the gate into forestry. Climb through woodland and heath for 1km to reach Captain Cook's Monument, towering above the escarpment. Best known for his Pacific voyages, explorer and navigator James Cook made the first recorded European contact with the east coast of Australia, as well as the Hawaiian Islands - where he was killed in a skirmish in 1779. He was born in 1728 in Marton, on the edge of Middlesbrough, and started his seafaring career in Whitby, but spent the defining years of his childhood at Aireyholme Farm south of Roseberry Topping, attending a charity school in Great Ayton which is now the Captain Cook Schoolroom Museum.

At the monument turn left, following the path through woods, scrub and heath. It eventually joins a track and carries on to meet a lane. Turn right here, retracing the outward route to Kildale.

Ingleby Incline

Distance 15km Time 4 hours Terrain good tracks, rough in places, and some quiet lanes Map OS Explorer OL 26 Access train to Battersby Station on the Middlesbrough to Whitby (Esk Valley) Line (around four trains daily)

The dramatic railway incline that carried ironstone from the mines of Rosedale rises steadily from the fields and woods of Ingleby Greenhow to the wide skies of the North York Moors. The reward of the climb is a panoramic walk along the edge of the escarpment, with the ghosts of former industry adding interest and atmosphere.

This walk starts from Battersby Station. A small car park is provided for train users, but there are also some roadside parking spaces available nearby. You could, of course, arrive by train.

From the station, follow the approach road through the small settlement of Battersby Junction to reach a T-junction. Turn right and, in another 400m, leave the road to turn left, following a side lane which heads resolutely towards the great northern escarpment of the Cleveland Hills and arrives at the house at Bank Foot.

Leave the lane here for a wide track, marked as the Moor to Sea Cycle Route, on your right. Its direct line and almost level profile are clues to its origin; this was the route of the Rosedale Ironstone Railway from Battersby Junction to the mines at Rosedale on the southern edge of the Moors. Follow its course, gradually rising into a great bowl below the Cleveland Hills. In just over 2km, the track forks at the foot of the Ingleby Incline.

The Ingleby Incline allowed trucks loaded with ironstone from the Rosedale Mines to descend 1.5km from the moorland plateau, pulling empties up in the opposite direction. It climbed nearly 250m in height on a gradient of one in five.

Bear left and climb the incline as it

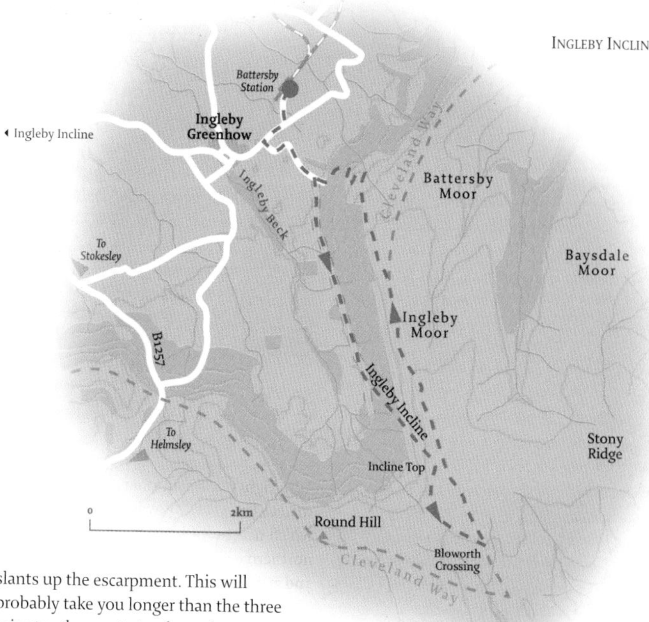

slants up the escarpment. This will probably take you longer than the three minutes the empty trucks took to conquer the slope! At the top, the track enters another world as it follows the course of the old railway across the wide heather-clad plateau of the North York Moors. (The route can be walked and cycled all the way to Rosedale, 15km from the incline top.) Now level, it is joined in around 1km by the Cleveland Way sidling in from the right, before reaching a major junction of tracks at the isolated site of Bloworth Crossing.

At this point leave the line of the old railway and turn sharp left, in company with the Cleveland Way, onto a wide track heading NNW. This climbs the moor and then skirts along the edge of the escarpment for the next 4km.

Where the Cleveland Way bears right at a signpost by a gate, leave the long-distance path and keep straight ahead. (As an alternative, it's possible to make a linear railway-linked walk by continuing to Kildale Station from here, following the Cleveland Way for 2km before joining a metalled road down to the village.)

A sandstone track, which is rough in places, descends Ingleby Bank, at first gradually and then more steeply. It twists left, then right as it prepares to meet the wooded foundations of the scarp at Bank Foot. From here, retrace the outward route to Battersby Junction.

The Wain Stones and Urra Moor

Distance 12km Time 3 hours
Terrain moorland paths, with some rocky sections; three significant climbs
Map OS Explorer OL 26 Access no regular bus service; check moorsbus.org to find out about any summer Sunday or Bank Holiday services

The northern escarpment of the Cleveland Hills rises abruptly from the pastoral country of the Leven Valley, topping out at more than 400m above sea level. In a few places the base rock extrudes through the peat and heather, nowhere more so than at the Wain Stones. On a misty day the shattered spikes of rock appear eerily out of the fog with little warning. On a clear day you will be rewarded by expansive views from the vantage point they create. This fine outing includes sections of remote moorland and significant climbing.

Start at the car park by the village hall at the southern end of Chop Gate. There are toilets here and a pub with a tearoom in the village. Turn left out of the car park and walk along the pavement past the Buck Inn. Shortly after passing the school, take the left turning, signed for Carlton in Cleveland, then immediately turn right behind the buildings to follow a bridleway, rising past the Methodist church on a narrow rutted track. Initially this may be overgrown and muddy, but within 1km it reaches the open moor. Continue through the gates and climb steadily through heather, the path later widening to a track along a broad ridge. Ignore any side turnings. After about 3km the ridge comes to an abrupt end on Cold Moor at a junction with the stone setts of the Cleveland Way. Turn right.

The long-distance path soon drops sharply to Garfit Gap. Keep straight ahead, ignoring any side paths, before climbing steeply to the atmospheric stone shards of

the Wain Stones. One of the oldest climbing venues in the North York Moors and popular since the first recorded ascent more than a century ago, the routes up the respective Stones go by such evocative names as the Steeple and the Needle, Sphinx Nose Traverse and Jackdaw Gully. For non-climbers, the path negotiates an easier way over the crags, before following the escarpment as a flagged footpath. It carries on over White Hill and eventually drops steeply to the road at the top of Clay Bank.

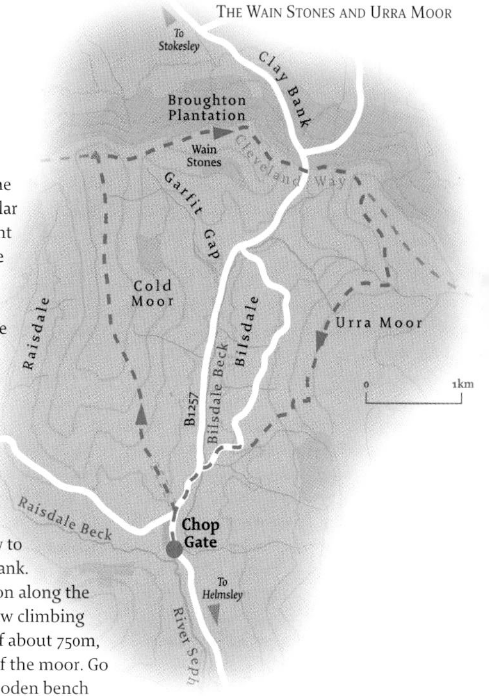

Cross the road and carry on along the Cleveland Way opposite, now climbing relentlessly for a distance of about 750m, before regaining the crest of the moor. Go through a gate next to a wooden bench to immediately reach a signposted fork in the bridleway. Leave the Cleveland Way here and bear right across heather and bracken on another bridleway. On this bleak moor, squawking pheasants have now given way to croaking grouse. Continue along the rim of the moor for about 3km, curving round the head of a small beck and ignoring side turnings for a bridleway and footpath.

A collection of three wooden signposts in close proximity heralds the turn-off. The first of these indicates a bridleway doubling back hard to the right, down a rather overgrown groove, to reach a gate. However, it will be better to avoid this reedy trench by simply turning at right angles along a small path next to the signpost. Very soon it arrives at the same gate. A clear route now heads down the side of the hill, becoming a wider track as it approaches Bilsdale Hall. When it comes to a lane, turn left to follow this back downhill to the road. Turn left and walk along the pavement through the village and back to the car park.

◂ The Wain Stones

Osmotherley by the Drove Road

Distance 13km Time 4 hours
Terrain woodland paths, moorland tracks; some road walking Map OS Explorer OL 26
Access bus (80/89) from Northallerton and Stokesley to Osmotherley

Osmotherley is set in a wooded hollow in the Cleveland Hills, tucked away from the A19 which carries traffic hurtling past the western edge of the National Park. It sits astride the Cleveland Way and is also the start point for the 64km Lyke Wake Walk, which crosses the Moors to Ravenscar on the east coast – it's no surprise then that this attractive village is a honeypot for visitors. This shorter challenge offers a taste of the Cleveland Way to start and finish, linked by a section of the ancient Hambleton Drove Road as it crosses the high ground on the edge of the moor.

From the centre of Osmotherley, follow the road uphill to the edge of the village. Turn left to follow the Cleveland Way along a track, Ruebury Lane, which climbs round the side of the hill and offers a wide panorama west as far as the Pennines. The track is bordered with hedges, colonised by gorse, holly and hawthorn.

At Chapel Wood Farm the track ends and the Cleveland Way continues as a footpath along the bottom of a field. It clings to the hillside and then enters South Wood. Immediately after the gate, bear right to keep on the long-distance path, striking uphill diagonally through a wide clearing between tall conifer trees. Towards the top it winds through an area of disused quarries to reach a level shelf amidst silver birch trees on the edge of Beacon Hill. Carry on along the edge of the escarpment, past a forest of transmitters and, further on, an obscure and secluded trig point hidden behind the wall on the right. The path later veers to the right and begins to descend, with views ahead towards the cone of Roseberry Topping.

At a gate, a bridleway to the right offers a quick return to Osmotherley, while the main route lies ahead through a second gate onto Scarth Wood Moor. After 1km

◂ Cleveland Way near Osmotherley

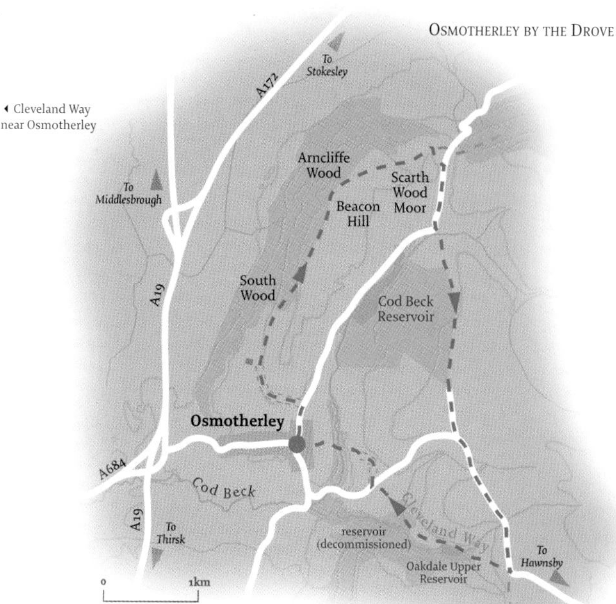

stay with this bridleway when it veers to the right to leave the Cleveland Way. However, this soon drops down to a road, where you turn right to walk alongside it until you reach a sharp right-hand bend after about 700m.

Leave the road here and walk straight ahead, crossing the beck on a footbridge and climbing some rocky steps up the track on the other side. This is the Hambleton Drove Road, followed for the next 3.5km across the moor. At a triangular road junction, keep straight ahead and follow the road for another 1.5km to Square Corner. At this point, the road takes a sharp turn to the left while the Drove Road keeps straight ahead. Instead of either of these choices, turn sharp right to follow a footpath signed for the Cleveland Way and Osmotherley.

The gravel and stone-sett path quickly drops down into Oakdale. Walk along the reservoir access path to Oakdale Upper Reservoir, then on through woodland before climbing to meet a road. Turn left and, after 100m, go right to continue along the route of the Cleveland Way up a green lane. In about 300m, watch for a stile and signpost in the hedge on the left. Cross the stile and follow the well-signed route down a small valley, across a beck and back up the other side into Osmotherley.

Arns Gill and the Head of Ryedale

Distance **9km** Time **2 hours 30**
Terrain **surfaced moorland tracks with a final section of quiet road walking**
Map **OS Explorer OL 26** Access **no regular public transport to the start**

The North York Moors include the most extensive area of continuous heather moorland anywhere in England. Although the land has been exploited for minerals, farming and forestry, there is little human habitation across the centre of the plateau. The atmosphere of space and wide horizons still endures, with little to break the silence beyond the croaking alarm of a grouse or evocative cry of a curlew. This straightforward moorland route follows excellent tracks around the head of Arns Gill, offering a taste of wild and remote upland.

Ryedale is the most westerly of the valleys to cleave the National Park. The Rye rises in the Cleveland Hills above Osmotherley before winding a course through Hawnby and Rievaulx and on to Helmsley. The moors are never far above, despite the wooded and pastoral trench the river drives through the wilder uplands. Arns Gill is one of the highest tributaries of the Rye, contributing its waters just 3km from the official source at Rye Head. Strictly speaking, it could itself lay claim to the title since it is the longest headwater in the Rye catchment.

A quiet moorland road traverses the upper reaches of Ryedale between Hawnby and Osmotherley. About halfway between the two villages there is a bridge over the Rye, the highest road crossing of the infant river. There is a small parking area next to it.

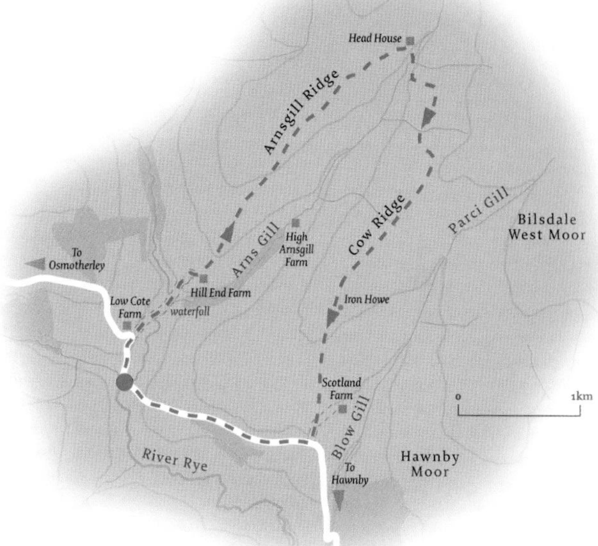

From the bridge, walk up the lane towards Osmotherley for about 400m to Low Cote Farm. Where the road turns sharply to the left, carry straight on along the farm road. Follow this concrete road downhill to the meadows bordering the River Rye. The track crosses the river, close to its confluence with Arns Gill, whose brief moorland journey ends with an impressive waterfall, seen to the right.

Over the bridge, the track climbs the other bank until it gains the top of the hill. Turn right at a sign for Chop Gate, keeping on the lane to Hill End Farm. Just in front of the farmhouse, turn left and keep with the track, now unmade, as it climbs steadily uphill. As it gains height, the track emerges onto open moorland across Arnsgill Ridge, a wide expanse of heather moor. The views are extensive, with the Bilsdale TV transmitter on the horizon. The sandy track continues for about 2km before reaching the remote cottage at Head House.

After passing an old cattle grid, the track twists down past the house and crosses Arns Gill. Climb up the other side of the valley, ignoring any side turnings as the route winds up the hillside before gaining a level course across the heather.

The return route stretches out before you for about 3km, riding the crest of Cow Ridge before gradually falling towards farmland and the Hawnby to Osmotherley road. Turn right to follow this for 2km back to the start.

◂ Head House, Arnsgill

The River Esk rises high on the boggy peat of Westerdale Moor and runs eastwards for nearly 32km to the North Sea at Whitby. It tumbles through pastoral, woodland and upland scenery, cleaving a route between heather-clad moors rising on either side.

A whole series of intriguing and enchanting side-valleys feed the river: Westerdale, Danby Dale, Great and Little Fryup Dale and Glaisdale. One of the most attractive railway lines in the country accompanies the river, calling at a sequence of stations serving the villages that straddle the valley and its tributaries: from the wild moor of Commondale to the bustling community of Grosmont. Here, the steam trains of the North Yorkshire Moors Railway join the conventional railway for the last few miles to historic Whitby. All the walks in this section can be started or completed at a railway station on the Esk Valley Line, or you could devise a linear route to link stations.

The Esk Valley

Upper Eskdale

Distance 14km **Time** 4 hours
Terrain outward route on good tracks; return by exposed moorland path, track and finally road. Careful navigation needed between Danby and Siss Cross **Map** OS Explorer OL 26 **Access** train to Commondale Station on the Middlesbrough to Whitby (Esk Valley) Line (around four trains daily)

This is a walk of two very unequal parts. The outer leg traces the enchanting upper reaches of Eskdale on good tracks. The return uses an ancient path to climb across wild moorland before striding across the crest of an exposed ridge. As this route links stations at either end, it could also make two linear walks.

If starting in Commondale village, take the road signposted to Castleton from the Cleveland Inn. (There is roadside parking in the village.) After about 300m, bear left up the station approach track. At the end of the drive, ignore the footpath down to the station on the right and instead carry on through a gate to follow a bridleway, part of the Moor to Sea Cycle Route. It's a good firm track, undulating along the valley side, with bracken and occasional isolated houses. There are grand views across the picturesque valley, with the railway track snaking towards Whitby. A line of oak trees marks the approach to the buildings at Winnow Hall; then the track climbs past a small conifer plantation to reach the road. Follow this downhill for about 200m. Immediately after the Castleton village sign, turn left up a bridleway signposted to Danby. Castleton Station and the Eskdale Inn are a little further down the road.

The bridleway is firm at first, but then becomes softer as it passes above a series of houses. On the opposite side of the valley, Castleton straggles along the top of a ridge, with the high moors rising beyond. Pass through a large silver birch wood where the route may be a little

◂ The bridleway near Commondale

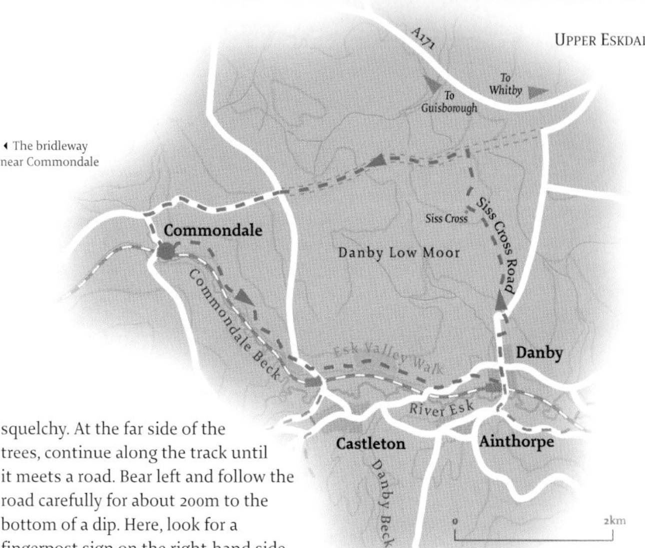

squelchy. At the far side of the trees, continue along the track until it meets a road. Bear left and follow the road carefully for about 200m to the bottom of a dip. Here, look for a fingerpost sign on the right-hand side, pointing out the Esk Valley Walk. Follow this footpath between fields and then houses before turning right to descend to Danby Station.

Turn left at the station. Walk up the road, passing the village green on the right (Danby village offers a café, pub and toilets), and continue straight over at the crossroads for the climb up the road opposite. About 100m after a cattle grid, bear right at a purple sign for a restricted byway, climbing this for about 300m to rejoin the road further on. Cross the road, but ignore the broad green track immediately ahead of you. Instead, turn right for just 10m or so and find a smaller grassy path on the left, parallel to the green track. Take this narrower path, which continues slightly above the green track for about 100m. It then bears slightly right, climbing gently and leaving its counterpart to a level course on the left.

The path rises gradually through grouse and heather moor for 2km or so. Its name, Siss Cross Road, may lead to exaggerated expectations. It is actually a rough and narrow path, though it's generally quite distinct. Care may be needed with navigation in places and it would be wise to use a compass in mist. Towards the crest of the path, you pass a grouse butt and then Siss Cross itself, a vertical marker stone to the left. The path weaves along to confront a broad stone moorland track after 300m. Turn left and take this across the crest of the moors with wide views on either side. In just under 3km, you come to a road junction. Carry straight on to follow the road down into Commondale.

Danby Beacon

Distance 10km Time 4 hours (one way) Terrain tracks, fields and country lanes, from valley floor to exposed moorland Map OS Explorer OL 27 Access train to Danby Station on the Middlesbrough to Whitby (Esk Valley) Line (around four trains daily); return by train from Lealholm

The Esk Valley Walk is a 60km waymarked route from Whitby to the source of the Esk on Westerdale Moor. This linear walk follows the section between Danby and Lealholm Stations, little more than five minutes by train but a bit longer on foot! It's a walk of two parts: the pastoral scenery of the Esk Valley followed by wild and exposed heather moor. Return by the scenic Esk Valley Railway.

From Danby Station, turn right and follow the road over the River Esk into Ainthorpe. Just after the bridge, bear left to follow a bridleway uphill a short way to another road. Go left and follow this quiet lane, the route of the Esk Valley Walk. In about 1km, pass a sports ground and pavilion on the right. Just after the next house turn left to leave the road, by a sign for Danby via the Moors Centre. Cross the railway line using the unmanned crossing (common-sense caution here!). Continue over the next field, crossing a footbridge, and reach a road by the Moors Centre. This is the National Park's excellent visitor centre in Danby Lodge, with an art gallery, shop, café and, for children, a climbing wall, play area, trails and activities. A short deviation will be tempting.

At the junction, turn right, passing the main car park on the left. After 300m, look for a gate and signpost in the hedge on the left. Cross the field diagonally and then pass along the top edge of the next field just below a wall, aiming for the upper side of the buildings ahead. A short section of often soggy lane passes between the farm buildings, after which a

◂ Danby Beacon

driveway leads to the road.

Carry straight on along the road for about 100m, then turn left up a walled track, again following the Esk Valley Walk. At the top of the track, cross the road and keep straight ahead, continuing to climb on the road opposite. In 300m, bear right to maintain the steady ascent to the junction at Danby Beacon.

From here, you can spot an array of human creations on the far horizons: to the southeast, Fylingdales Early Warning Station; to the north, Boulby Potash Mine; to the west, Captain Cook's Monument. These are reminders, in turn, of this landscape's strategic importance, industrial legacy and ability to inspire adventure and shape world history. The Beacon itself (perched on top of a tumulus, or ancient burial ground) marks the location of a radar station which operated through World War II and the Cold War, but the far-reaching views mean there has been a warning beacon on this moorland as far back as the Middle Ages.

At this point, take the track, originally a road, signposted to Lealholm, and follow this for about 3km. The moor is dotted with all sorts of historic relics and, on this section alone, the route passes another tumulus and the base of a cross on the left. After about 3km, at a junction of tracks, take the right branch, signposted with the Esk Valley Walk (leaping salmon) logo. After about 400m, join a road and continue downhill into Lealholm.

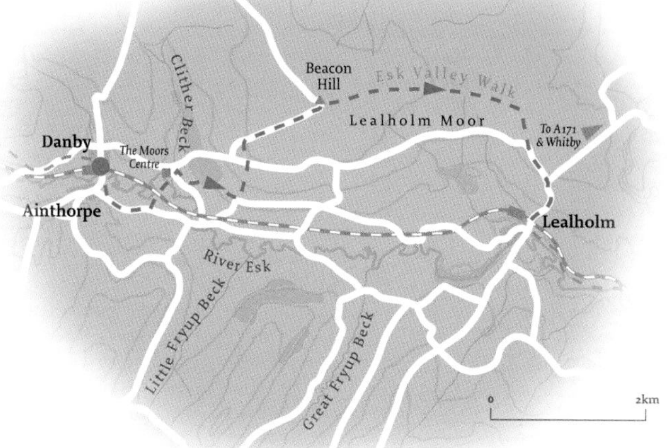

Above Danby

Distance 6km Time 2 hours Terrain intricate route of hillside paths and lanes Map OS Explorer OL 26 Access train to Danby Station on the Middlesbrough to Whitby (Esk Valley) Line (around four trains daily)

The stone houses and red-tiled rooftops of Danby offer a colourful welcome. This route explores the hillside to the north of the village, returning via the National Park's Moors Centre and the valley floor. Although quite intricate, it presents no major navigation problems. The walk is described from Danby Station, but an alternative start point would be the Moors Centre, a former shooting lodge set in an idyllic position next to the river (parking charge) with a shop, gallery and café set in gardens.

From Danby Station, turn sharp left next to a footpath sign to Castleton. Pass the Methodist Chapel, climbing past some cottages on the left. The stone-sett path continues beyond the houses to join the road. Turn left and follow this with care, down and then up for about 400m. At the beginning of some open land, look out for a track bearing right. (There's a bridleway sign set in the side a little way back from the road.) Follow this, the Esk Valley Walk, with views across the valley to Ainthorpe. After about 500m there's a small post marking a junction of tracks.

Leave the Esk Valley Walk here, as it continues ahead towards Castleton. Instead, bear right to climb the grassy hillside. The path soon follows a wall and levels out through bracken. It's boggy in places, before becoming a walled greenway for a short stretch. At the end of the greenway, you come to a track crossing. Instead of turning along this in either direction, take a fainter path ahead, bearing slightly to the right and cutting off the corner of the field. This soon brings you to a wall with woodland beyond. Just in front of this, go through a

◂ Water bailiff statue by the River Esk

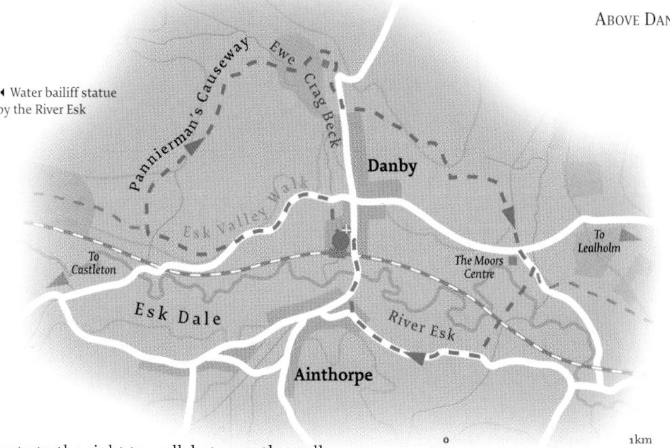

gate to the right to walk between the wall and fence – this is part of a 12th-century monastic route known as Pannierman's Causeway. The path leads downhill into a small wooded valley, crossing two becks, one with stepping stones and the other by a footbridge. Climb the next field towards the house at Rosedale Intake, continuing past the buildings and along the approach track to join a road.

Turn right and take the road downhill for a short distance. You can shorten the walk here by continuing on the road back to Danby village. Otherwise, immediately before the cattle grid and next to a sign, turn left along a broad track. This climbs around the rim of the hillside above Danby, across a bracken-covered slope. At the top of the hill, just before a wall at a junction of tracks, leave the main track and turn right to go downhill on a broad grassy path. There are various tracks and paths here, but the simplest route is to descend for about 300m to a gate. Then turn left and carry on downhill, with the wall on your right, dropping quite steeply to a gate in the corner of the field. Go through this to turn right along the top of another field. Pass through a further gate and descend through woods to the road.

Cross the road ahead and pass the Moors Centre on the right. Just beyond the Centre, bear right to follow the Esk Valley Walk below the play area and on across the River Esk on a footbridge. After another field, come to an unmanned level crossing over the railway. Although there are no more than eight trains a day passing this point, it is wise to avoid intimate acquaintance! Continue up the track on the other side to join the road. Turn right and follow the country lane to the village of Ainthorpe. When the road bends sharply to the left, leave it and continue straight ahead down a short section of bridleway. At the bottom, turn right and follow the road over the River Esk into Danby.

Glaisdale and the rocky roads

Distance 15km Time 4 hours
Terrain mostly lanes and tracks rising to exposed moorland Map OS Explorer OL 27
Access train to Glaisdale Station on the Middlesbrough to Whitby (Esk Valley) Line (around four trains daily)

Around Glaisdale and Egton, the River Esk is set in pleasant broadleaf woodland with the open moors above. This route explores both realms, climbing out of the valley to loop into the heather-clad hinterland. Although there is a lot of road walking, it is on quiet, unfenced lanes sweeping over the broad crest of the moors,with panoramic views extending to the sea.

This walk starts at Glaisdale Station. There are parking spaces near the railway viaduct, downhill from the station. Turn left from the station and walk downhill towards the viaduct. Ahead, through the arch, is Beggar's Bridge, erected by local man Thomas Ferris in 1619. The story goes that, as the son of a poor sheep farmer, he was refused consent to marry Agnes, daughter of the local squire, so in 1586 Thomas went to sea to make his fortune, before returning to marry her. On the night of his departure, the Esk was in spate and he was unable to cross the river to bid her goodbye. He commissioned the rebuilding of the bridge after her death, recalling how the river had separated them.

Just before the viaduct, turn right to cross a footbridge, by a ford, over the Esk, then climb the steps on the far side. At the top, turn left to take the route of the Esk Valley Walk, rising through oak and beech woodland. It's also the route of Alfred Wainwright's Coast to Coast Walk.

The attractive pathway leads along the hillside above the River Esk. Further on, it parts company with the river and continues as a broad track through mature woodland until it comes to a road. Turn left downhill here. In about 500m, at the bottom of the hill, turn right to leave the road and take a public bridleway, the access track to Grange Head Farm. This crosses a bridge and a pleasant hedge-lined track

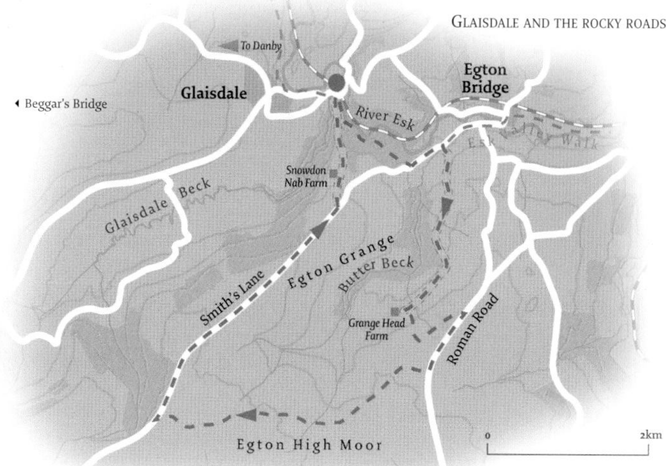

climbs steadily between fields and woods. Further up, the landscape becomes rougher, with views of the high moors. The valley of Butter Beck lies down to the right.

About 2.5km after leaving the road, the track turns sharp right to approach Grange Head Farm. On the corner, leave the track and turn left through a gate. A right of way climbs the enclosure. The route isn't obvious, though a marker post guides you part of the way up. Soon you can see the fence along the top; aim for the stile. Cross this and, in about 30m, you meet a thin path parallel to the fence. Follow this left, with views to distant Whitby and the sea. This rough path runs a little way from the fence and wall, before gradually curving round to join a road.

Turn right along this quiet, unfenced moorland road which follows the line of a Roman route between a fort at Lease Rigg, near Grosmont, and a camp to the south at Cawthorne, near Pickering. In 750m, leave the road and turn right, taking a track past a barrier. Follow this for 4km as it weaves an almost level route across the vast, open expanse of heather moor.

When it comes to an end at a road, turn right and follow this for about 3km. Enjoy being on top of the world, with panoramic views and virtually no traffic. Later, the red roofs of Egton add colour to the hillside across the Esk Valley, while the sea glints in the far distance. Just before a cattle grid, pass a small tumulus, William Howe, on the left. About 1km beyond the grid, turn left down a narrow no-through road. This soon curves to the right, opening up a broad vista of Glaisdale. Beyond the house at Snowdon Nab, the lane becomes a rutted track, shaded by bushes, trees and giant ferns. This descends through woodland to reach the ford and the station at Glaisdale.

A spell on the Goathland Rail Trail

Distance **6km** Time **2 hours (one way)** Terrain **excellent track along disused railway line** Map **OS Explorer OL 27** Access **train to Danby Station on the Middlesbrough to Whitby (Esk Valley) Line; North Yorkshire Moors Heritage Railway to return from Goathland to Grosmont (timetable varies according to season)**

The magical Rail Trail follows the line of George Stephenson's original railway, opened in 1836. Initially, carriages were pulled by horse and hauled up the Beck Hole Incline by wires. Steam replaced horses in 1845, but a fatal accident on the incline led to the rerouting of the railway. The replacement route is still followed by steam trains of the North Yorkshire Moors Railway. This gentle and accessible stroll through the country of the Murk Esk Valley rewinds from the bustle of Grosmont junction to the moorland station of Goathland, famous for its big-screen role in *Harry Potter*.

Starting at the main Grosmont Station buildings, go over the level crossing to the signalbox, then cross the road to a tarmac path which passes in front of a row of cottages. Don't go straight ahead through the tunnel entrance to the engine sheds; instead, bear left to climb over the hill. A sign marks the start of the Rail Trail, which goes up to the left-hand side of the tunnel, then crosses back over the portal. There are great views of the 1960's scene, with semaphore signals and traditional steam trains. After crossing the tunnel, turn left through a gate signed for the Rail Trail to Goathland. The route now passes above the engine sheds and down by the sidings and the line of the railway as it heads up the valley of the Murk Esk.

A wide cindertrack continues ahead, following the line of the original Stephenson railway. The present North Yorkshire Moors Railway soon veers away to the left on the far side of the small community of Esk Valley, while the Rail

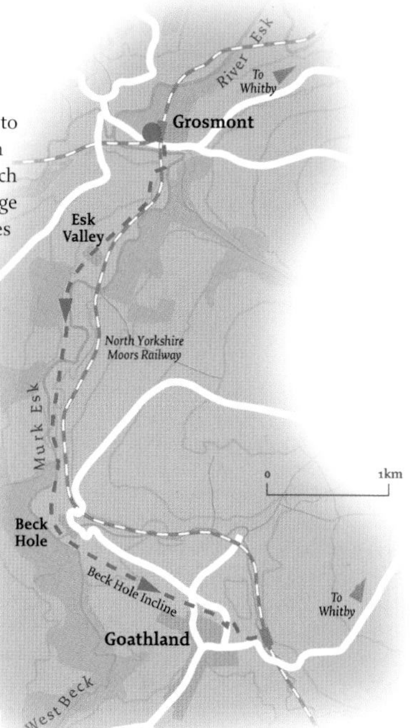

◂ Goathland Station

Trail continues straight ahead, passing to the right of the cottages. Soon the open floor of the valley gives way to oak, beech and ash trees, as the route skirts the edge of Spring Wood. A wooden bridge carries the trail across the Murk Esk before the route steams ahead above open meadows along an embankment. With the present steam railway now well up the hillside to your left, all sign of it is out of view - unless you spot the steam from a passing engine. The track passes through woodland and later accompanies the river before approaching Beck Hole, at the confluence of Eller Beck and West Beck, the two headwaters of the Murk Esk. (Beck Hole is a charming waterside hamlet which is worth a detour. The picturesque cascade at Thomason Foss lies a short way east of the settlement and there are also views across the steam railway as it winds along the valley of Eller Beck.) The houses are to the left, but the track passes through the site of the original station. Cross Eller Beck and continue through the grounds of Incline Cottage before climbing the Beck Hole Incline.

At the top of the incline, cross a road and continue beyond as the final section ascends a grass clearing into Goathland. The moorland village is well known as the setting for the TV series, *Heartbeat*, as well as the location for Hogsmeade Station, a stop on the line of the Hogwarts Express in the *Harry Potter* films. Not surprisingly, it is a magnet for sightseers and coach tours.

At a second road crossing, you can turn right to explore the village. Otherwise, to reach the station, turn left and walk along the road for about 50m. Turn right through a kissing gate to follow an unsurfaced private road, the Mill Green Way. At the end of this, turn downhill to reach Goathland Station.

Mallyan Spout and Eller Beck

Distance 10km Time 3 hours
Terrain tracks and good paths, but steep sections; rocky approach to Mallyan Spout with a precipitous edge on return path
Map OS Explorer OL 27
Access train to Goathland on the North Yorkshire Moors Heritage Railway

This circuit explores the moorland around the tourist honeypot of Goathland. It visits the pleasant upper reaches of Eller Beck and the hidden wooded chasm of West Beck. The highlight is the secluded waterfall at Mallyan Spout.

From Goathland Station, go through the gates from the Pickering (southbound) platform. Turn right and follow the footpath rising steeply behind the station. At the top, pass a seat and join a broad grassy track, following this to the right. Shortly, branch left, climbing to the right of a row of houses to reach a road.

Turn left to follow the road for about 30m, then go right along a no-through road. This lane contours through the bracken above the valley of Eller Beck. It curves round to cross a small clough, then climbs up to a cattle grid, where it becomes a bridleway.

Turn left in front of the buildings at Partridge Hill Farm and take the bridleway downhill, crossing the beck by stepping stones. Veer to the right and continue above Birchwood Farm to join an access track beyond the buildings. Follow this track for about 700m until it meets a road. Walk along the road under the railway bridge, then up past a cattle grid. Just in front of the cottages, turn right through a gate for Sadler House. Take the bridleway, a broad cindertrack which follows the line of George Stephenson's 1836 railway. This was later replaced by the present route of the North Yorkshire Moors Railway.

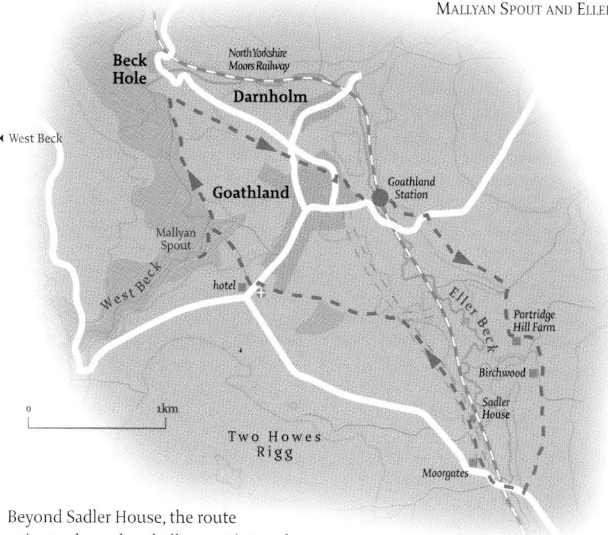

Beyond Sadler House, the route continues through a shallow cutting and, after 1km, comes to a track crossing next to a campsite. Turn left here, following a signpost for Mallyan Spout. Skirt the left-hand side of the camping field to go through a gate hidden in the far left corner, continuing on the path beyond, across a duckboard and then a footbridge. The route passes along the edge of a sequence of fields before emerging in the south end of Goathland village, near the church.

Cross the road and take the footpath just to the right of the Mallyan Spout Hotel. A good surfaced path drops steeply down to West Beck, with steps in places. On reaching the beck, you can turn left to walk a short distance to Mallyan Spout itself, negotiating the boulders with agility and careful footwork. Otherwise, turn right and follow the right-hand side of the water towards Beck Hole. A well-surfaced path soon climbs out of the ravine and follows the top edge of a precipice. Later, a long flight of steps leads back down to the valley, joining the former rail track at Incline Cottage. To explore the charming hamlet of Beck Hole with its inn and views over the steam railway, turn left here. Otherwise, turn right and climb up the incline on the line of the track.

At the top of the incline, cross a road and continue beyond as the final section ascends a grass clearing into Goathland. At a second road crossing, turn left and walk along the road for about 50m. Turn right through a kissing gate to follow an unsurfaced private road, the Mill Green Way. At the end, turn downhill to reach Goathland Station.

Ruswarp and the Esk Estuary

Distance **5km** Time **2 hours**
Terrain **riverside paths, with some town walking** Map **OS Explorer OL 27**
Access **train to Ruswarp Station on the Middlesbrough to Whitby (Esk Valley) Line; local bus services**

This circular link between Ruswarp and the historic fishing port of Whitby follows the Monk's Trod and the cindertrack on a high-level route into town. The return traces the final mile of the tidal Esk back to Ruswarp, passing beneath two great viaducts. There is plenty to explore in Whitby itself, with its harbour, abbey and seafront – not to mention its links with *Dracula* and all things Gothic.

From Ruswarp Station, turn right to follow the road towards Whitby, with the church on your left. In about 300m, just between a butcher's shop and the Ruswarp Hall Hotel, turn right along a small ginnel. This is easy to miss, but there is a sign for the Esk Valley Walk, with its leaping salmon symbol. The flagstone path, the Monks' Trod, leaves the village and crosses the meadows on the Esk floodplain, passing through a wetland area.

At the far side, a flight of steps takes you up to a junction of paths. Keep straight ahead, following a sign to Whitby Marina and the cindertrack. The path weaves along the top of a steep bank, below some allotments, before steps lead down to a broad track, once a link between the high- and low-level railways through Whitby.

Turn left for a gradual climb. Later join the cindertrack, sidling in from the right. This is the old railway from Scarborough to Whitby, now a cycle route. A short tunnel takes it under the main road. In another 300m, it ends and steps on the right bring you down to the road.

Walk down the hill with the majestic

◂ Whitby

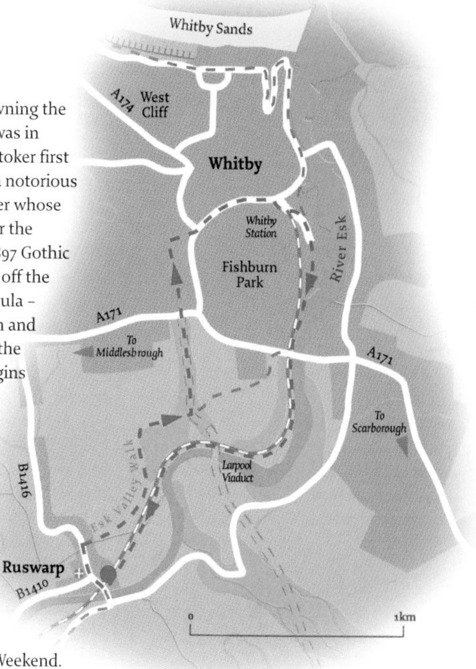

ruins of Whitby Abbey crowning the horizon in the distance. It was in Whitby that author Bram Stoker first came across a reference to a notorious 15th-century Romanian ruler whose name he swiftly adopted for the eponymous villain in his 1897 Gothic novel, *Dracula*. Shipwrecked off the Yorkshire coast, Count Dracula – an East European nobleman and vampire – comes ashore in the guise of a black dog and begins a campaign of terror in the town. References to local history, folklore and landmarks, including the abbey, are woven into the plot, and today Whitby's links with literature's most famous vampire are much in evidence around town, especially during the established Whitby Gothic Weekend.

Cross a busy road junction to Bagdale and follow this all the way down to Whitby Station. (You could go down through Pannett Park if you prefer.) Turn right after the station onto Langborne Road. This passes the harbour office and Marina car parks. At the far end, head to the right of Coates Marina and take the 'Railway riverside path to Ruswarp', which squeezes between the marina buildings and the railway, then goes under the modern roadbridge. Beyond, the route follows the tidal estuary upstream between the railway and the riverside yards. Rounding a bend, dive beneath the massive red-brick arches of the Larpool Viaduct, dating from the 1880s. This carries the cindertrack on the line of the railway between Middlesbrough and Scarborough. Continue on the path, now more open with good views of the river and, later, Ruswarp Church. A raised embankment takes the path along its final section to Ruswarp.

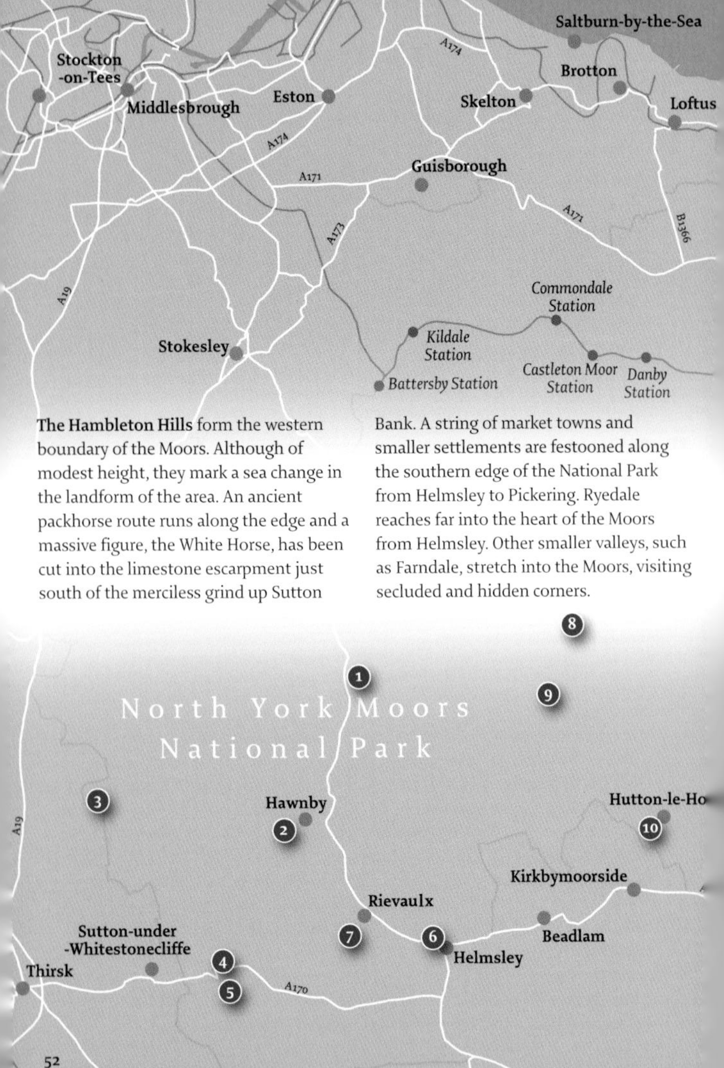

The Hambleton Hills form the western boundary of the Moors. Although of modest height, they mark a sea change in the landform of the area. An ancient packhorse route runs along the edge and a massive figure, the White Horse, has been cut into the limestone escarpment just south of the merciless grind up Sutton Bank. A string of market towns and smaller settlements are festooned along the southern edge of the National Park from Helmsley to Pickering. Ryedale reaches far into the heart of the Moors from Helmsley. Other smaller valleys, such as Farndale, stretch into the Moors, visiting secluded and hidden corners.

Ryedale, Hambleton and the Southern Dales

▲ East Mines, Rosedale

Bilsdale highs and lows

Distance 7km **Time** 2 hours 30
Terrain field and moorland tracks. One significant climb **Map** OS Explorer OL 26
Access no regular bus service; check moorsbus.org to find out about any summer Sunday or Bank Holiday services

The River Seph rises close to the northern edge of the North York Moors but flows south, carving out the pastoral valley of Bilsdale, a wide trench between the moorland on either side. The community of the dale is scattered along its length from the village of Chop Gate to the confluence of the Seph and the Rye by Newgate Bank. Bilsdale's parish church is set, not in a village but on the main road, close to the hamlet of Fangdale Beck, and it's where this walk starts. The route uses bridleways to explore the fields and woodland in the valley itself, with a high-level moorland section skirting the dale's edge.

Parking is available in a small lay-by next to Bilsdale Parish Church, around 5km south of Chop Gate on the B1257 between Stokesley and Helmsley. Cross the road and turn down a small lane, signposted to Fangdale Beck only. Entering the hamlet, keep left, passing a converted chapel. Stay on the lane as it bends to the left and then ends at the farm buildings of Malkin Bower. Keep straight ahead past the farm, going through a gate onto a bridleway. The route is waymarked, and follows the valley of the River Seph, first on a track and then through a sequence of fields. A track continues beyond the manicured grounds of Helm House, weaving through fields near conifer plantations and oak trees, the

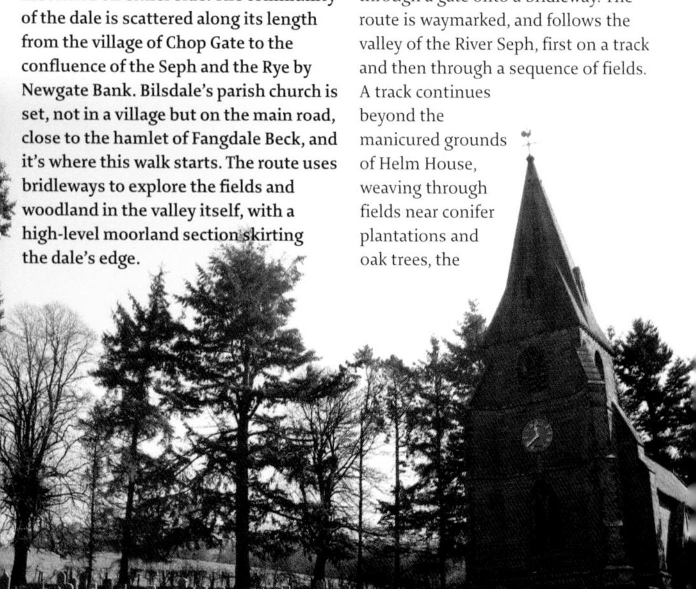

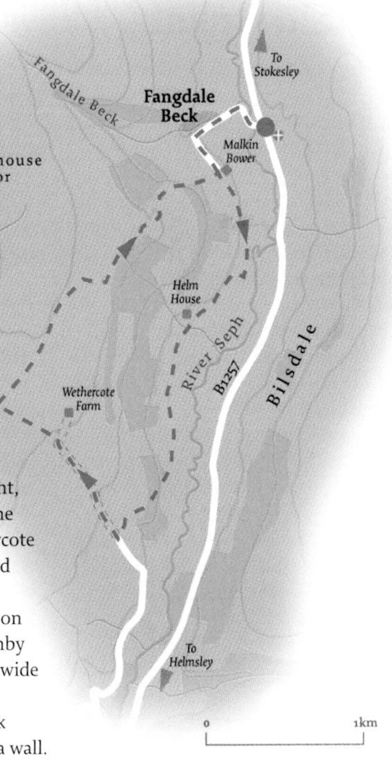

sound of pheasants never far away. Coming to an open field, the route of the bridleway divides, but it's not very evident on the ground. Watch out for the start of a grass track slanting uphill towards a gate on the lower edge of the conifer plantation. Once you've seen the gate, the route is clear, with a wide track climbing the hillside through the plantation and beyond.

When you come to a lane, turn right, ascending again. In less than 1km, the lane bends right to approach Wethercote Farm. On the bend, leave the lane and turn left to a bridleway. This climbs alongside two fields, before arriving on the open moor. To the left, the Hawnby Hills dominate the foreground with wide views across the head of Ryedale.

Turn right and follow a sandy track along the edge of the moor, next to a wall. In just under 1km, the track bears left across the moor. At this point, keep straight ahead, staying near the wall and taking a smaller, but clear, cart track through the heather. This roughly follows the line of the wall, turning right downhill and then left across the top of a plantation. Soon after the end of the trees, you come to a gate in the moor wall. Leave the moor here and continue downhill. The track is a deeply-rutted trench and it's easier to walk along its rim, soon passing through old quarry workings. The track becomes broader and leads downhill, now more steeply, until it reaches Malkin Bower. Turn left and follow the lane through Fangdale Beck to the start.

◂ Bilsdale Parish Church

Around Hawnby Hill

Distance 9km Time 3 hours Terrain tracks and paths across fields and moorland Map OS Explorer OL 26 Access no regular public transport to the start

Hawnby Hill is a small but dramatic outlier of the Tabular Hills. Its craggy sides and sharp ridge draw the eye, offering a modest but satisfying challenge. The walk extends from the hill to make a circuit above the valleys of Ladhill Gill and the River Rye.

Parking in Hawnby village is very limited, so the best place to start is a small parking area near Hawnby All Saints Church, about 1km west of the village. From the lay-by, walk up the lane away from the church. In 200m, at a signposted road junction, turn right to climb uphill towards Hawnby.

In about 400m, opposite a farm, turn left by a footpath signpost. A good track leads on through fields, with the tree-clad slopes of Hawnby Hill rising up to the right and the wooded valley of the Rye down to the left. In about 1km, you pass the isolated Hill End House. Just beyond it, at a junction, keep straight ahead, signed 'Bridleway to Moorgate'. About 300m further on, watch out for a grassy trail leaving the main track and veering to the right round the end of Hawnby Hill. Follow this, climbing to the saddle of the hill.

At this point, turn right and look for a small path climbing diagonally up the left-hand side of the steep ridge. Follow this through bilberry and heather to reach the summit ridge. The path continues along the sharp edge of this narrow and airy ridge. Bracken and a variety of hardy trees cling to the steep rock-strewn sides. On reaching a small well-made cairn, enjoy the views, then retrace your steps to the track at the base of the north end of the hill.

From here, turn right to follow the track down to a road, with the bulk of Easterside Hill dominating the foreground. To shorten the walk and return direct to Hawnby, turn right here and follow the

quiet road back to the village. Otherwise, turn left to follow the road for a few metres, before finding a sign by a gate on the right: 'No vehicles, except for access'. It is unclear what kind of vehicle would be able to navigate the old byway, but it is certainly a passable pedestrian route. Follow the sunken path down the side of a field, across a marshy area and through some light woodland to a footbridge across Ladhill Beck. The original route crossed the beck on a ford just to the left, but a footbridge is a better option now. On the far side you have to negotiate some unavoidable marsh, keeping left around the undergrowth to pick up the byway at the ford a few metres upstream.

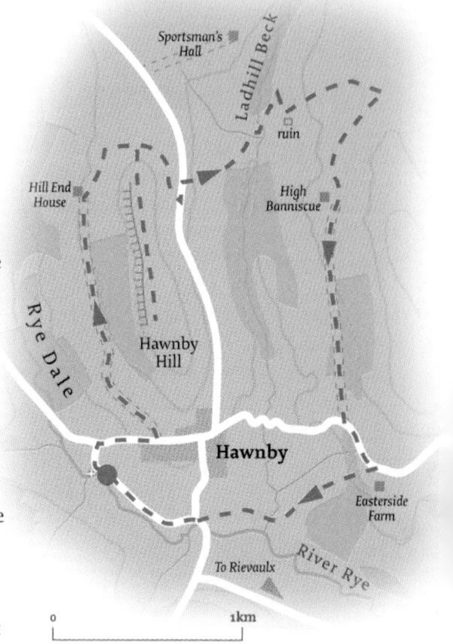

At first, this runs parallel to the beck, but soon it climbs diagonally up rough pasture. In about 200m, turn sharp right, doubling back at a crossing of tracks with the profile of Hawnby Hill now clear across the valley to the right. Keep to the left of a ruined building and find a gate in the fence just behind it. Beyond the gate, follow a sunken pathway winding up through heather. On approaching a wall to the right, with Easterside Hill behind, watch out for a small path crossing the track. Take this to the right to reach the wall, following it a short way further to reach a five-bar gate.

Go through the gate and cross a small marshy area to a second gate on the right. Turn left through this and follow the top side of the next two fields. Just before the farm buildings at High Banniscue, follow the signs to take the bridleway on an avoiding route, just up to the left of the farm. Regain the approach road on the far side.

Continue along this pleasant track across the side of Easterside Hill and through conifer woodland to reach a road in about 1km. To reach Hawnby direct, you can turn right here. Otherwise, turn left and follow the lane. Immediately before Easterside Farm, turn right at a public footpath sign. The right of way goes diagonally down the field, through a small patch of woodland and down another field to a footbridge. Cross this and continue, emerging at a road junction near Hawnby Bridge. Carry straight on along the lane, passing a tearoom and shop, to return to the start.

◂ Near Hawnby Bridge

Kepwick and the Drove Road

Distance 7km Time 2 hours 30
Terrain hill paths, forest and moorland tracks and a quiet lane; an initial climb
Map OS Explorer OL 26 Access no regular public transport to the start

A rewarding climb from attractive Kepwick leads to the ancient Hambleton Drove Road across the Moors. This parallel route to the Great North Road was used for moving thousands of cattle between Scotland and the south of England until the 19th century, following the edge of the Hambleton Hills.

There is a small car park near the church in Kepwick. Walk up the road past the church. In about 200m, turn left through a gate by a public bridleway sign. It may be muddy on the other side, but it does get better! Climb up the field; the official route of the bridleway follows the line of trees. At the top of the field, go through the gate and bear left.

The path climbs the hillside above Kepwick village, later weaving through a forest of rhododendron bushes on a clear rutted path. Once through the bushes, escape onto the open grass spur of

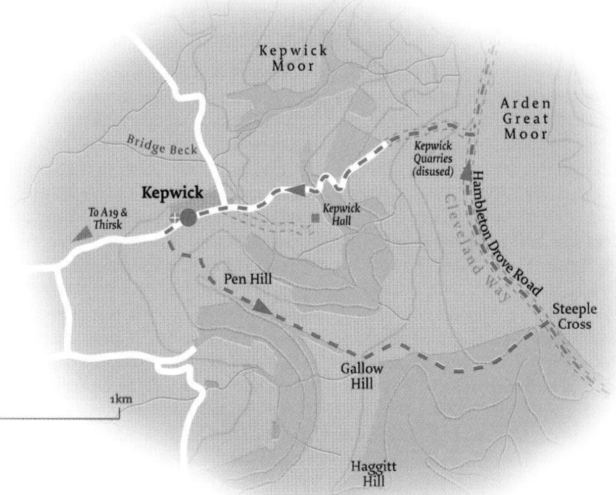

ˀen Hill. Now level, continue straight ahead on a broad grass path running parallel to the wall. It heads for a gap between two groups of trees ahead.

At the end of the open heath, pass through a gate into a strip of silver birch woodland and follow the route near the left-hand wall. At the end of the wood, the path rises and veers left to follow a narrow gully, before coming to a gate in front of a plantation.

Go through the gate into the forest and keep straight ahead at the crossing of bridleways. Soon sidle into a wider track, and carry straight on through the plantation, ignoring any side turnings. Later the route levels out, curving round to a junction with a major track running north-south beyond the boundary of the forest. This is the Hambleton Drove Road, also part of the Cleveland Way.

Turn left here. On the right is Steeple Cross, a small ancient boundary stone. Continue along the broad Drove Road across heather moors for 1.5km.

This brings you to a junction of tracks at the terminus of a tarmac lane. Turn left, passing through a gate. Walk down the lane as it weaves through the disused and grassed-over workings of the extensive Kepwick Quarries. Beyond these, the lane winds downhill through woodland, passing the grounds of Kepwick Hall, until it returns to the village itself.

◀ On the Hambleton Drove Road

Garbutt Wood and Gormire Lake

Distance 5km **Time** 1 hour 30
Terrain woodland paths with some steep gradients **Map** OS Explorer OL 26
Access no regular bus service; check moorsbus.org to find out about any summer Sunday or Bank Holiday services

Gormire Lake is the only natural lake in the North York Moors National Park and only one of three of any size in the whole of North Yorkshire: the others, Semer Water and Malham Tarn, are both in the Dales. Gormire lies in a wooded hollow, scoured out and dammed by the last ice age, with no obvious source or outflow for water which just permeates the rocks and filters out through the hillside. The tranquillity and beauty of Gormire's natural amphitheatre is hidden by the broadleaf trees of Garbutt Wood, draped down the hillside to the water's edge.

The start is at Sutton Bank National Park Centre, where there is a car park (charge), information centre, exhibitions, a café, toilets and picnic tables.

From the back entrance to the National Park Centre, walk across the grass area and reach the A170, just where it dives over the edge of Sutton Bank. The perils of the hill for HGVs and towing vehicles are notorious, and caravans are banned from even attempting it. Just here, a sign points the way to Sneck Yate via the Cleveland Way. Follow this into the woods and along the edge of the escarpment.

In about 500m, leave the long-distance footpath to turn left at a sign for a footpath and nature trail. Drop steeply down the bank towards Gormire Lake below. The path slants diagonally through Garbutt Wood Nature Reserve, managed by the Yorkshire Wildlife Trust and

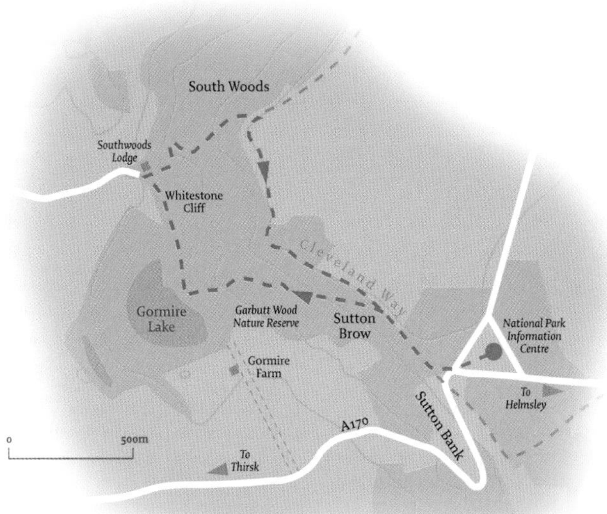

omprising deciduous woodland of eech, oak and birch, with holly, hazel nd mountain ash. The trees attract a ariety of birdlife, including the brightly-oloured bullfinch and the aptly named reecreeper, which scours its way from he bottom of the trunks to the top ooking for appetising insects.

Keep on the path, ignoring side urnings and continuing relentlessly ownhill until you arrive at Gormire Lake, et in a sylvan dell. At the water's edge, urn right, following the sign to South Voods. The bridleway continues past the ake and on through woodland, where ou will encounter many holly trees. Up o the right, you might glimpse the rocky crags of Whitestone Cliff looming dramatically above the trees.

Arrive at a T-junction of paths marked by a fingerpost. Turn right here, following a bridleway quite steeply uphill on a sunken path, which is muddy at times. It's a steady climb and the path follows a zigzag course, but as you gain altitude the way gets drier and the gradient more merciful. Ignore turnings and carry straight on up. At the top of the hill, you emerge from the woods to a junction with the Cleveland Way which runs across the top of the bank. Turn right here to follow the level path across the top of the cliffs and back to the National Park Centre.

Whitestone Cliff

The White Horse

Distance 5km Time 1 hour 30
Terrain well-surfaced, level track and woodland paths; steps around the Horse
Map OS Explorer OL 26 Access no regular public transport to the start

The elevated plateau of the North York Moors rises abruptly from the Vale of York. Its west-facing profile is the great limestone escarpment of the Hambleton Hills. Nowhere is this more dramatic than at Sutton Bank where the main road clambers up the slope at a gradient of 1 in 4. At the top, the gateway to the park is marked by the National Park Centre, the start point for many walks. This route follows the cliff south for a close encounter with the Kilburn White Horse, the most northerly turf-cut figure in England.

At 100m long and 70m high, the White Horse was financed by local businessman Thomas Taylor and built by local schoolmaster John Hodgson and his helpers in 1857. During the Second World War, it was camouflaged for fears that the bold equine totem would serve as a navigation aid for Nazi bombers. Now, its idiosyncratic outline poses proudly on the hillside, visible for many miles to the south and west.

The start is at Sutton Bank National Park Centre, where there is a car park, information centre, exhibitions, a café, toilets and picnic tables. From the rear of the visitor centre, take the path signposted to the White Horse. Cross the busy A170 as it surmounts the edge of Sutton Bank and follow the Cleveland Way on the opposite side, marked by the white acorn icon. Immediately, a wide panorama lies at your feet with views across the Vale of York to the hazy purple outline of the Pennines beyond. Gormire Lake is tucked away in woodland at the foot of the slope. Ahead, the escarpment forms a great crescent of limestone, culminating in Roulston Scar.

Continue along the well-surfaced path as it follows the edge of the cliff. In a while,

◂ On the path to the White Horse

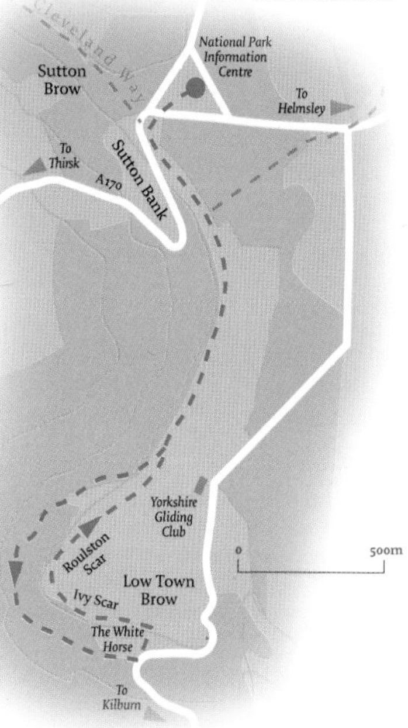

you pass the grounds of Yorkshire Gliding Club, where German pilots trained with gliders when Germany was denied an air force during the inter-war years. With the pilots gaining such intimate knowledge of the terrain and the landmark White Horse, fears that it would threaten the North's security if visible were well grounded. When you're nearly level with the club's buildings across the runway, there's a board on the left describing its history and activities. At this point, bear right diagonally down a narrow path known as the Thieves' Highway. (If you prefer to reach the White Horse on the main all-ability path, continue straight ahead.)

The Thieves' Highway slants down through woodland. At the bottom of the hill, keep straight ahead and join a broader forest track. This contours round the base of the escarpment through mixed woodland with its carpet of bluebells and forget-me-nots in late spring and the cliffs of Roulston Scar soon towering above to the left. The track arrives at a small parking area and road. Just before the road, turn left up the steps by a stone post with details about the Kilburn White Horse, which looms above and to the left. At this close quarter, its appearance is of amorphous grey limestone scree, though you can make out its hind leg if you concentrate hard enough! Although a full view of the Horse is better gained from a distance, there is nothing like seeing the enormous profile emerge out of the scree above the forest. A stone carving records that £100 was originally invested to provide 'the triennial grooming of the figure'; such grooming is ongoing to prevent the horse retreating back into the landscape. The route climbs steeply to the right of the Horse's rear quarters, mostly on steps. At the top, the path bends left, levels out and continues above it. A clear and level return route lies along the escarpment path, passing between the vertiginous edge of Roulston Scar and the main runway of the gliding club, before joining the outward route from Sutton Bank.

Abbot's way from Helmsley

Distance 10km **Time** 4 hours (round trip) **Terrain** excellent undulating path following the Cleveland Way **Map** OS Explorer OL 26 **Access** buses from York, Malton and Pickering to Helmsley

Helmsley is a medieval town built around its broad marketplace, with a Norman castle dating from 1186. Although largely destroyed in the English Civil War, substantial buildings remain and are now in the care of English Heritage. This walk follows the first pleasantly undulating section of the long-distance Cleveland Way which shares an historic pilgrims' route to the ruined 12th-century Rievaulx Abbey.

There is a large car park (charge) near Helmsley Castle. The start of the Cleveland Way is marked by a stone sculpture, engraved with some of the place names encountered on the route. There is also a signpost indicating a stone track, bordered by hedgerows, rising gently out of town, with views of the castle on the left. Just beyond the castle is the five-acre walled garden, dating from 1759 and now run by a charity, with a shop and tearoom (seasonal opening).

Continue along the edge of two fields. A hard surfaced path leads on past a gate, going left and then right between a field and woods. On the southern side of the woodland lies the private 18th-century house of Duncombe Park, the ancestral home of the Duncombes, whose senior member takes the title Baron Feversham. A Gothic memorial to the second Baron stands in Helmsley's town square.

Soon, a steep descent brings you into the cleft of Blackdale Howl, though its watercourse is just a diminutive ditch. Climb the steps on the other side and continue through light woodland. This is

◂ Rievaulx Bridge

now limestone terrain, with hawthorn, bramble and rosebay willowherb. A mix of oak, ash, and conifer colonises the ground and the path inclines gently uphill to open land. Cross the driveway to Griff Lodge, keeping straight ahead across the top of Whinny Bank. The views ahead now encompass the flat-bottomed valley of the Rye, weaving through woodland.

A gradual descent heralds the approach to Rievaulx, with a stony track passing through pleasant woodland to meet a road. Turn left and follow the footpath just above the road as it drops down to the broad flat pastureland at the bottom of Ryedale. Where the walkway ends, follow the road for about 500m, with the evocative ruins of the abbey rising up across fields to the right. Rievaulx's most influential Abbot, St Aerled who, during his term, presided over some 650 monks and laymen, first reached the abbey along this route from Helmsley Castle.

Just before the 18th-century Rievaulx Bridge, at a road junction, turn right along the lane to reach the abbey after 600m. This English Heritage site is open to the public (charge for non-members), as is the National Trust's Rievaulx Terrace on the hillside above (charge for non-members). Retrace your steps to the start.

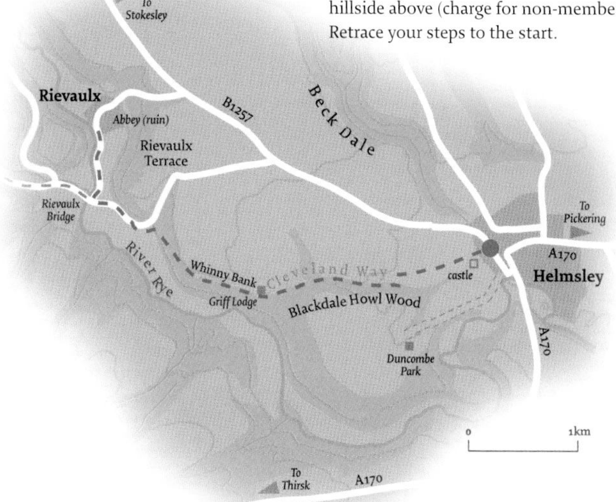

A Rievaulx pilgrimage

Distance 4km Time 1 hour 15
Terrain paths and lanes with no serious ascent Map OS Explorer OL 26
Access check moorsbus.org to find out about any summer Sunday or Bank Holiday services

The haunting ruins of Rievaulx Abbey are impressive enough, a reminder of the days of monastic wealth and spirituality. But the setting makes them truly magnificent, built in a natural amphitheatre between the steep and wooded sides of Ryedale. This walk is an easy circuit of the valley around Rievaulx, including woodland, meadows and ancient bridges.

The Cistercian community at Rievaulx was founded by Normans in the 12th century (its name originating from *Rievalle* or 'Rye Valley' in French) and became one of the richest and most successful monasteries in the North of England. At its peak, more than 600 men worked and lived here, including monks and lay brothers. Sheep farming was a major source of income with flocks spread across the neighbouring dales. Fishing was also an important enterprise and the remains of ponds can still be seen. The abbey's ironworks continued to operate even after the monastery was suppressed in 1538. High above the abbey sits the Rievaulx Terrace, created with a Classical temple at either end for the Duncombe family who incorporated Rievaulx into their parkland in the 1750s. The Terrace and temples are in the care of the National Trust.

There is a car park (charge) at the abbey and very limited roadside parking in the

◂ Rievaulx Abbey

village. From the abbey car park, turn right and walk through the village as far as the parish church. Opposite the church, turn left along a lane. This climbs gently out of the village and heads along a terrace above the valley. At a fork, take the unsurfaced lane on the left downhill, glancing back at the ruins which so inspired Romantic artists, including JMW Turner. A pleasant, hedge-lined track returns to the valley floor and crosses the Rye at Bow Bridge.

Cross the bottom of the valley and, when the track begins to curve uphill to the right, leave it and turn left through a gate. The public footpath is signposted for Ashberry and leads through the flat meadows along the bottom of the valley. After a couple of fields, the path climbs into Ashberry Wood, now contouring above the River Rye. It curves around the slope of Ashberry Hill through ash and beechwoods. At a fork, keep left along the lower path to skirt the edge of the wood with a view across the watermeadows of the valley floor, then continue to a road at Ashberry Farm. Keep left to cross a bridge, then turn left along the road signed for Rievaulx. After about 400m, this crosses the River Rye. Turn left after the bridge and follow the road back to the abbey.

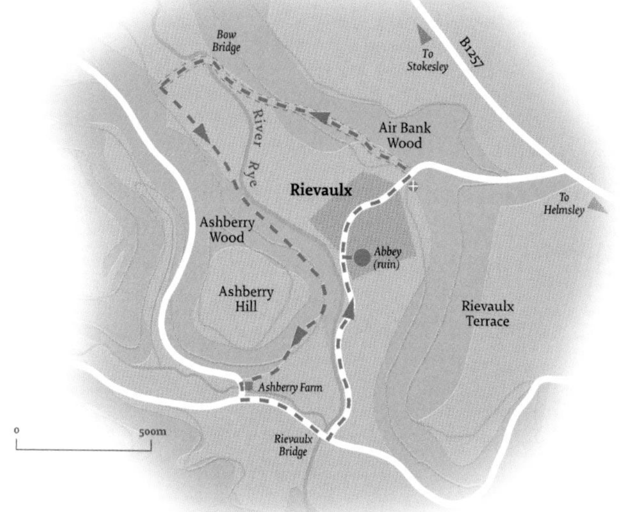

The Rosedale Railway

Distance 14km **Time** 4 hours 30
Terrain clear tracks and paths through exposed moorland and rough pasture
Map OS Explorer OL 26 **Access** no regular bus service; check moorsbus.org to find out about any summer Sunday or Bank Holiday services

The Rosedale Railway was completed in the 1860s to serve the ironstone mines of the dale, and stretched for 22km from the East Mines to Battersby Junction to the northwest. Though the line closed in 1929, much of the fascinating industrial architecture remains. The bed of the railway, a permissive path, offers a lofty vantage point with great views as it trundles around the head of the dale.

Start from the small roadside car park on the Castleton to Hutton-le-Hole road at Blakey Junction, about 500m south of the Lion Inn. A footpath is signed to Rosedale from the road here. It soon comes to a broad level track – the bed of the Rosedale Railway. Turn left to follow the course of the railway which you can make out as it curves right round Rosedale towards the lines of kilns on the opposite side. Pass the remains of a brick watertower before the track sweeps round the head of the dale. The wide cindertrack gives way to a rougher path tracing a route through old workings, and, depending on season, the brown, green and purple of the heather.

The path crosses the infant River Seven on a massive embankment before resuming its long loop around the valley side, now heading south. Its height has gradually dropped since leaving Blakey Junction and the Lion Inn is clearly visible back across the valley. Some 5km from the start, pass the Nab Scar loading dock and another long embankment. Later, the track approaches the East Mines. The first remains include a huge stone structure, which contained the 'iron kilns' in which the ironstone was heated. Later, the remains of the 'stone kilns' are evident as a row of arches. After the kilns the track widens into the terminus of the line, now occupied by miscellaneous farm relics and paraphernalia. Here, you come to a gate at the far end.

Follow the track past a farmyard down to the road at Hill Houses. Turn right and follow the road for about 200m, then turn left down a driveway by a footpath sign for the River Seven. Pass a series of houses – mostly holiday homes – and then a farmyard. Continue down the right-hand side of the next two fields, before crossing a footbridge over the River Seven. The climb up the often boggy field on the far bank brings you to a track.

Turn right and walk along this track, known as Daleside Road, for about 2km, with views back across the valley to the remains of the East Mines. Pass to the right of a terrace of buildings and keep going along the track, which here comprises a walled lane through the rough pastureland at the bottom of the valley.

Coming to a lane, turn left, soon passing through the buildings at Moorlands Farm. Continue on the lane until the tarmac ends at a gate. Keep straight ahead. A track climbs steadily for 1km through bracken slopes to reach the line of the tramway. When you reach this, turn left and follow it for about 400m to reach the short footpath connection on the right. This leads back to the car park.

◂ Ironstone railway

Farndale Daffodil Walk

Distance 6km **Time** 2 hours (round trip) **Terrain** riverside path – surfaced and mostly level **Map** OS Explorer OL 26 **Access** no regular public transport to the start

The Farndale Daffodil Walk is a Yorkshire tradition. Some believe the daffodils were first planted by medieval monks from Rievaulx. Whether this is legend or not, they are a popular attraction today, and deservedly so.

Because of the need to protect the flowers, the Farndale Local Nature Reserve was established here in 1955. Come between mid-March and mid-April for a spectacular display stretching for miles along the banks of the River Dove. Inevitably, this is also a busy time for visitors and car parks, so it's worth choosing a weekday if you can. The River Dove is a lovely setting for a walk at any time of year, especially in May for the bluebells, and the valley's position between the high moorland on either side makes it all the more enchanting.

This walk follows the line of the waymarked route from Low Mill to the hamlet of Church Houses, a distance of around 3km. There are alternative return paths, but none better than the outward route – with a different perspective on the dale in either direction.

Start at Low Mill car park, which has toilets and an overflow car park (charge). Take the public path signposted to High Mill and follow this down to cross the River Dove on a footbridge. The path along the other side is well-surfaced and level, with a series of gates. At first it passes a small cliff on the far side of the river. Soon it continues across a series of small fields alongside the water, before passing a small wetland area on the right. Depending on the season there are plenty of other flowers besides daffodils, including ramsons and bluebells. One section climbs a little way above the riverbank through some woodland.

After about 2km, the route passes between the buildings at High Mill, one of which houses the seasonal Daffy Caffy. Beyond High Mill, follow the access lane to the small settlement of Church Houses. Refreshment is also available here at the Feversham Arms. The little church of St Mary lies just beyond the hamlet, about 500m up the lane to the right.

The best route back is the way you've come, though there are alternative field paths and lanes to return to Low Mill.

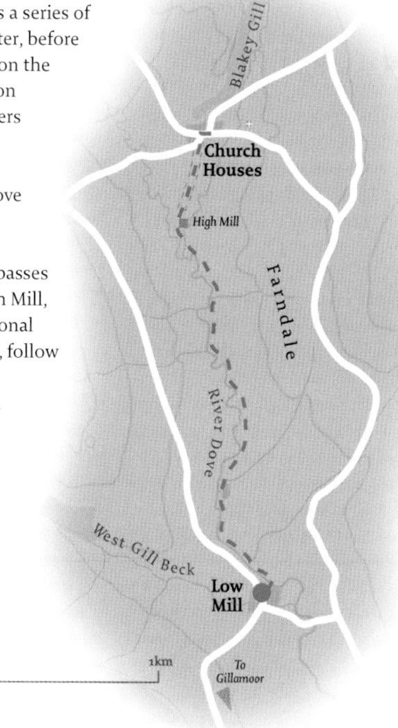

◂ St Mary's Church in Church Houses

Douthwaite Dale to Hutton-le-Hole

Distance **9km** Time **3 hours** Terrain **tracks and paths through woods and fields, hilly in places. One section of busy road** Map **OS Explorer OL 26** Access **regular bus (128) from Scarborough and Helmsley to Kirkbymoorside, 3km from the start**

Hutton-le-Hole is one of the most popular villages around the Moors, tucked into a small valley with a clear limestone beck weaving a route between the houses scattered along its village green. Peaceful in contrast, lofty Gillamoor crowns a ridge overlooking the River Dove. This circuit visits both villages and explores the hidden, wooded valley of Douthwaite Dale. The final 1km section is along a road which can be busy.

The best start point is the parking area 1.5km south of Hutton-le-Hole along the road towards Kirkbymoorside. Walk south beside the road towards Kirkbymoorside for about 200m. Just after the cattle grid take the rough lane to the right, marked for Douthwaite Dale only. Follow this down into the valley to reach the River Dove just above a weir, an idyllic spot for the riverside houses. Cross the footbridge and continue on the lane which climbs up the wooded bank opposite before levelling out at the top. Where the lane comes to a sharp left-hand bend and T-junction, turn right to follow the side road towards High Park and Low Park Farm.

In about 700m, when the lane turns sharply to the left, keep straight ahead on a track between hedgerows. The route runs along the rim of Douthwaite Dale, with a steep wooded slope dropping sharply to the River Dove below and a contrasting scene of arable fields stretching away to your left. On the second (left-hand) twist of a double bend, leave the main track and bear right to follow a signed public bridleway, known as the Shepherd's Road, into the forest. Descend through sycamore and beech woodland and, later, through a conifer plantation. Ignore side turnings

◂ Hutton-le-Hole

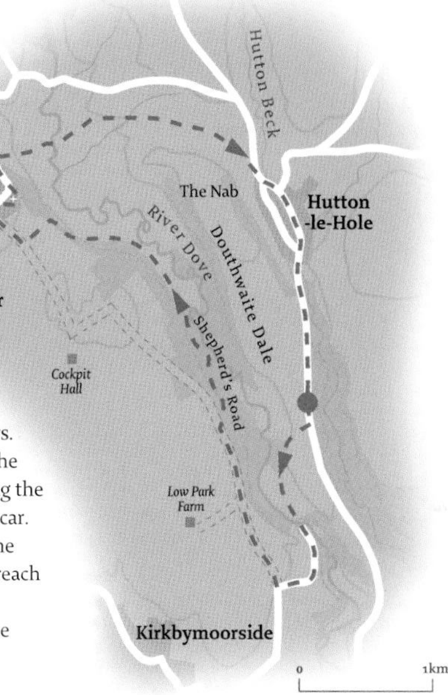

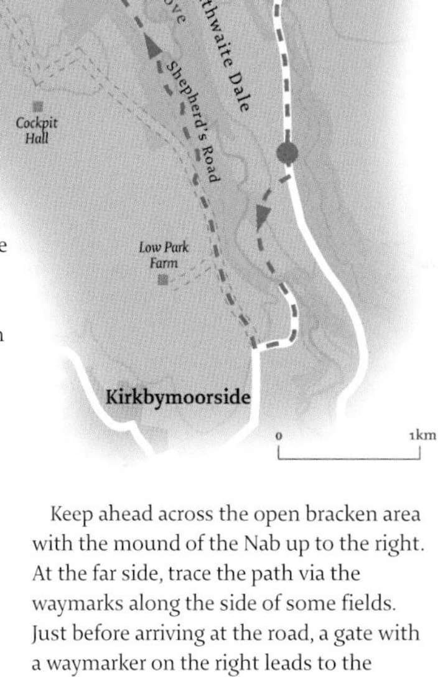

and stay on the track as it keeps dropping through the trees.

Towards the bottom of the valley, sidle into another track and keep straight ahead, ignoring any side turnings. An occasional waymark confirms you're on the right route as woodland gives way to valley meadows. After a while, climb back up through the woods (it can be muddy here), reaching the top of the bank by a small limestone scar. Follow the bridleway markers out of the wood and across a few small fields to reach a gate onto a lane. Turn right here and continue into Gillamoor, coming to the village green and Royal Oak pub.

Turn right to follow the main street, then take a footpath to the right of the church. Follow this downhill and around the back of the church to reach a lane at the bottom. Turn sharp right here along the byway. The track approaches mill buildings at the bottom of the hill. A waymark/signpost directs the path around to the left of the buildings and across the footbridge on the other side. Waymarks then guide you through the next few fields, passing just below a farm and then crossing a footbridge. Climb a few steps to a track, turning left and, very soon, right to find the path continuing up the fern-covered bank.

Keep ahead across the open bracken area with the mound of the Nab up to the right. At the far side, trace the path via the waymarks along the side of some fields. Just before arriving at the road, a gate with a waymarker on the right leads to the public right of way around a few houses and into the village of Hutton-le-Hole. Turn right and walk through the village.

The only realistic return to the start is to walk alongside the road for 1km or so. Although it's an unclassified road, it can be fast and busy, so care is needed where the verge disappears.

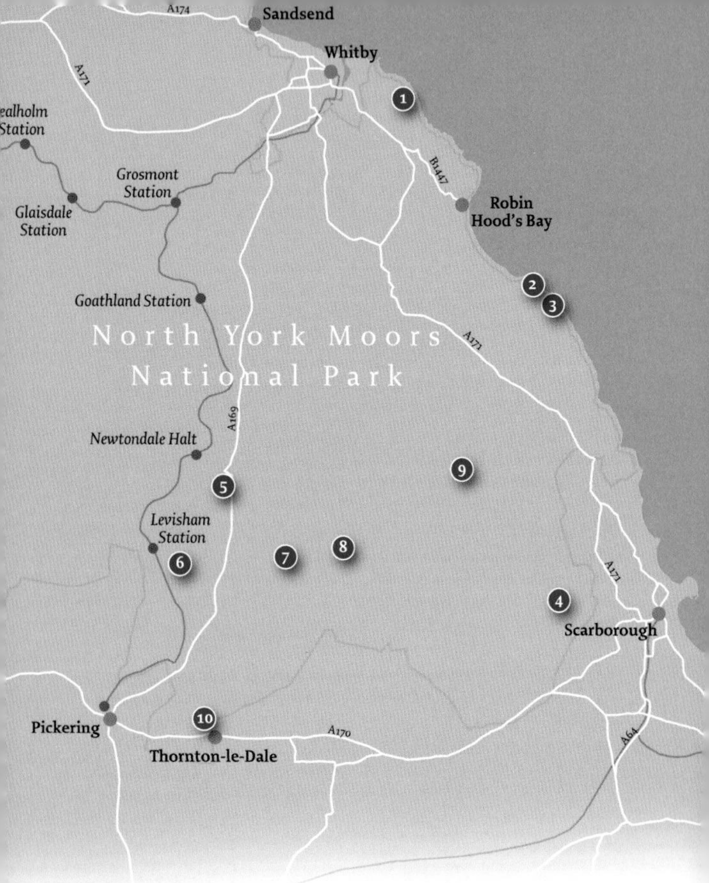

The eastern side of the National Park includes extensive areas of woodland, known collectively as the North Riding Forest. The most popular is Dalby Forest, with more than 300 hectares of trees stretching across ridge and dale. To the west, the deep clefts of Newton Dale and the Hole of Horcum pierce the moorland plateau and invite exploration. In contrast, the east coast between Whitby and Scarborough offers an unspoilt line of cliffs facing out across the North Sea.

Near Stoupe Beck Sands ▸

North Riding Forest and the East Coast

Whitby and Robin Hood's Bay

Distance **21km** Time **6 hours**
Terrain **undulating coast path, with significant climbing. Return route along old railway track** Map **OS Explorer OL 27**
Access **regular bus (93) from Robin Hood's Bay and Scarborough to Whitby**

Enjoy magnificent views on this clifftop hike from Whitby, a lively seaside town with darker undertones as partial setting and inspiration for Bram Stoker's *Dracula*. Behind the sandy beach and picturesque houses of Robin Hood's Bay, too, lies a shady past as a smugglers' haven. Return on the bed of the coastal railway that once ran to Scarborough. An alternative to the full circuit is to return by bus to Whitby.

Start from Whitby Station. There is a car park nearby (charge). Head for the harbour and cross the swing bridge to the east side. Turn left along Church Street with its mix of tourist and specialist shops. At the end, keep to the right and climb the 199 steps – a popular tourist challenge in itself – to the abbey. At the top, pass the parish church on the left and then the ruin of the historic abbey to the right – a landmark for many miles, guarding the entrance to Whitby Harbour and the mouth of the Esk.

Go through the car park and join the road on the far side, shortly turning left along the signed tarmac path of the Cleveland Way. After the last houses, this follows the cliff edge between farmland and the precipitous sandy crag below.

Pass through a caravan park, the rocky promontory of Saltwick Nab jutting out into the sea. At the far side of the site, go through a gate and take the clifftop path. In 1.5km, pass a giant fog signal, perched on a single-storey dwelling. The foghorn – combined, in season, with hundreds of kittiwakes nesting below – make it unlikely this would be a quiet retreat! Soon the path passes behind the lighthouse at Whitestone Point.

Beyond here, the route makes a switchback over the dramatic clifftops, with

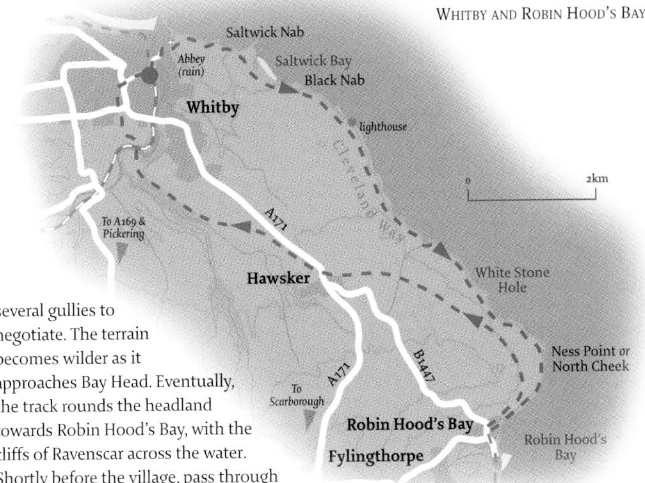

several gullies to negotiate. The terrain becomes wilder as it approaches Bay Head. Eventually, the track rounds the headland towards Robin Hood's Bay, with the cliffs of Ravenscar across the water. Shortly before the village, pass through Rocket Post Field. Post such as the one found here were used to fire a line with lifesaving equipment to ships in trouble. Pass some houses before arriving in the village, for some the end of the marathon Coast to Coast Walk. Though Robin Hood's Bay has no known link to the romanticised outlaw with whom it shares a name, it has an alluring, if murky, history of its own – as a smuggling haven, in which the whole community was complicit, with such a network of converted cellars and cupboards that it was said 'a bale of silk could pass from the bottom of the village to the top without seeing daylight'. To explore Robin Hood's Bay, carry straight on.

To return to Whitby, turn right on the path signed for the cindertrack and head uphill beside a couple of houses. Shortly, turn right onto the track itself to follow it for about 5km to Hawsker. This is the line of the former coastal railway between Scarborough and Whitby, now a cycletrack for almost the whole of its length. Although the gradient is tame for walkers, it is steep for a railway and would have been a piston-wrenching pull for steam engines negotiating this bank. The route alternates between lush cuttings and embankments, with great sea views. Soon after the track levels out, it crosses the main A171 at Hawsker village.

Shortly afterwards, pass a cycle centre and café next to the track. A long gradual descent to Whitby follows, with the abbey and town visible across fields to the right. Approaching Whitby, a high-level viaduct carries the track across the Esk Valley. The final section is mostly in a wooded cutting. At the end, some steps lead down beside the bridge to a road. Go downhill, cross a busy road junction to Bagdale and follow this all the way down to Whitby Station.

◂ On the coastal path

Coast trail from Ravenscar

Distance 7km **Time** 2 hours 30 **Terrain** good coast path and disused train track **Map** OS Explorer OL 27 **Access** bus (115) from Scarborough to Ravenscar

Ravenscar is perched on spectacular cliffs, with a panorama of great natural beauty – but it was not always like this. The village was once the focus for industry, especially alum and brick-making. Quarries and other remains recall the day when this coast was a hive of industrial activity. In the early 1900s, Ravenscar was also the site of an ambitious tourism project, and the network of roads built to accommodate a flood of visitors can still be traced. It could never rival Scarborough, however, and the project wilted after the company went bankrupt on the eve of the First World War. After exploring the old alum works, follow the Jurassic coastline to Stoupe Beck Sands. The high-level return is along the disused coastal railway, now a cycletrack.

Start at the National Trust Visitor Centre in Ravenscar village, where there is also a car park. Perched high above the sea, the views are glorious, stretching across to Robin Hood's Bay. A broad, well-surfaced track drops downhill from the road corner at the entrance to the car park. It heads towards the sea through a mix of broom, gorse and rowan, before sweeping inland (left) across the golf course. A concrete track then takes you across rough grassland, falling gradually towards the sea, until you come to a junction with the Cleveland Way. For a short walk, you could turn sharp left and follow the Cleveland Way back up to the visitor centre. Otherwise, keep straight ahead. In about 100m, turn right at a signpost, leaving the main track and following the coast path (still the Cleveland Way) as it loops down around the disused alum works. Alum was in demand in the textile industry, where it was used to embed the dye into cloth. The

◂ The Cleveland Way near the old alum works

path weaves on beyond the ruins, down and up a gully, across a field and then over a footbridge to reach a junction.

Turn right here, keeping with the Cleveland Way. The coast path now finds its way down to the cliff and traces the edge for just over 1km. The sheer cliffs of Bay Ness and the red rooftiles of Robin Hood's Bay frame the horizon. When the path comes to a small lane, turn left. (To walk to the legend-soaked Boggle Hole with its youth hostel set in an old watermill and the popular Robin Hood's Bay, both smugglers' haunts, carry on along the coast path for another 3km.) Climb the lane, aiming for a great bowl in the hillside, gouged out with quarry workings. The road becomes increasingly steep. Just after a double bend, and before a bridge, leave the road for a gravel track to the left. This joins the cindertrack on the bed of the Whitby to Scarborough Railway. Its route lies along a hillside terrace, with commanding views across the coast. Later, in a more sheltered section, it curves below old quarry workings and brickworks, now colonised by trees and shrubs. The hotel and houses of Ravenscar are perched on the clifftop ahead. The track continues up to the visitor centre and road corner at Ravenscar, with the Cleveland Way joining for the last few metres.

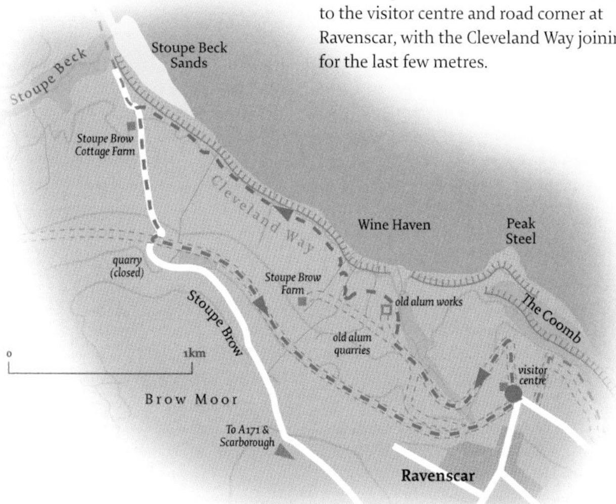

Ravenscar and the War Dike

Distance 6km **Time** 2 hours
Terrain a gentle coastal walk which leads near cliff edges **Map** OS Explorer OL 27
Access infrequent bus (115) from Scarborough to Ravenscar

Ravenscar lies at the summit of the old coastal railway line, which opened in 1885. From the north, the gradient was 1 in 39, nearly the steepest possible hill for a friction locomotive. The community has been an industrial centre and the focus for a failed attempt as a designer resort, when plans for an ambitious tourist project were aborted just before the First World War. Today, it makes an atmospheric and scenic base for exploring the coast. This is a leisurely walk, but passes near the edge of precipitous cliffs.

Start at the National Trust Visitor Centre in Ravenscar village, where there is also a car park. From the road corner by the visitor centre, head southeastwards along Station Road for just over 100m. Then turn left along a very broad track heading towards the sea and marked with the Cleveland Way sign. When it comes to the edge of the cliff, it turns right to follow the clifftop, still on the Cleveland Way. Soon, to the right, pass a car park and nearby tearoom – this will be useful to remember for later! Keep straight ahead along the coast path. The scene opens up in front, with the dramatic cliffs above Rocky Point and the seaboard stretching south past Scarborough to Filey Brigg. This is one of the best coastal sections of the Cleveland Way,

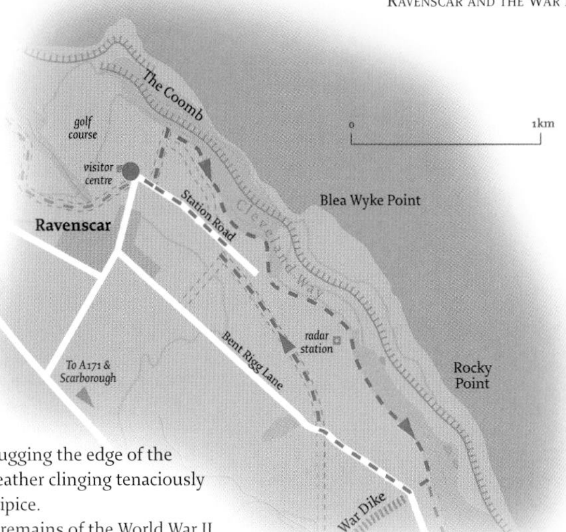

the path hugging the edge of the cliff and heather clinging tenaciously to the precipice.

Pass the remains of the World War II radar station, a collection of several brick buildings, which include the barrel-roofed communications hut, now preserved as an ancient monument and in the care of the National Trust. Carry on for another 1km until you come to a fingerpost.

Leave the coast path here, turning right across a stile. Follow a permissive path along the edge of one short field to reach a lane. This is the site of the War Dike, an earthwork which formed a medieval estate boundary, known as the Steindic. It marked out land granted to the Knights Hospitallers of St John of Jerusalem in at least the 12th century. The junction also lies precisely on an invisible national grid boundary dividing Great Britain into north and south. North of here grid references are preceded by the letter 'N', to the south 'S'.

Turn right to follow this tranquil cul-de-sac. In about 600m, watch out for a gap on the left, just before you cross a bridge. The gap leads on to the cindertrack, a cycleway following the line of the old coastal railway. Turn right and follow this back towards Ravenscar. The route rises gradually, passing the upper edge of the radar station seen earlier. A permissive path allows exploration of the preserved site. In season, wildflowers garnish the sides of the track, among them bird's foot trefoil, harebell and clover. The track ends at the platform of the old Ravenscar Station, next to the car park and tearoom, a height of 192m above sea level. Go down the steps, past the tearoom and then turn left along Station Road back to the start.

◂ Coast and flowers

Raincliffe Woods and Forge Valley

Distance 10km Time 3 hours
Terrain woodland and field paths, some steep climbs Map OS Explorer OL 27
Access bus (128) from Scarborough and Helmsley to East Ayton, where you can join the route at Seave Gate Gill 1km away

Raincliffe Woods is a patch of mixed woodland, offering a range of popular alternatives to the coastal walks around nearby Scarborough. The adjoining Forge Valley carves its way through the limestone buttresses of the River Derwent. Together, they form a Site of Special Scientific Interest while Forge Valley is also a National Nature Reserve.

Start at Green Gate car park, 3km north of East Ayton, along a minor road through the Forge Valley. Take the bridleway on the left from the car park and follow this through mature mixed woodland for just under 2km. After a patch of open ground, re-enter the woods and keep on the main track, ignoring all side turnings. Where a smaller path continues straight ahead, rising steeply, follow the main path left. Climb to the top of a hill, arriving at a rough T-junction just short of an old boundary fence. Turn left here – a broad way descends steeply through the trees. At the bottom, it emerges by the small glacial lake of Throxenby Mere. Turn right along the road for a few metres and then, very shortly, turn right again along a lane.

Where the lane bends left after passing a yard, keep straight ahead up a bridleway signed for Row Brow. It's a clear track, though it can be muddy in places, rising steadily through the trees. Further up, watch out for glimpses of Scarborough to the left. The climb ends abruptly at the brow of the hill, next to some masts. Bear right, past the transmitters, and take the access track beyond.

The fields around here are host to a myriad of tumuli and earthworks. To the left, Seamer Beacon is crowned with a small copse. After just over 1km, the track merges into a road next to some barns. Turn right here and follow the bridleway,

◂ Sculpture in Raincliffe Woods

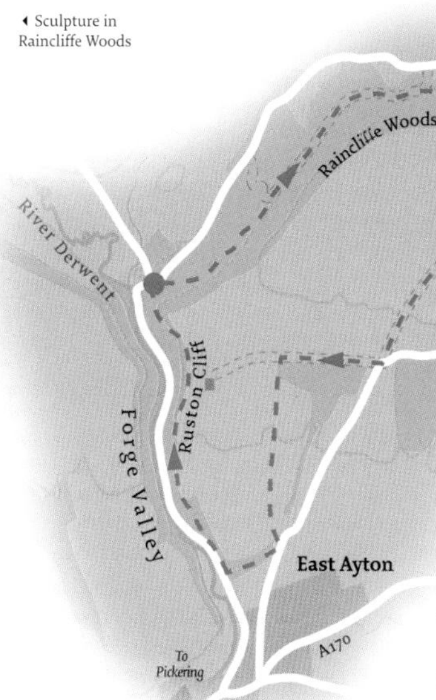

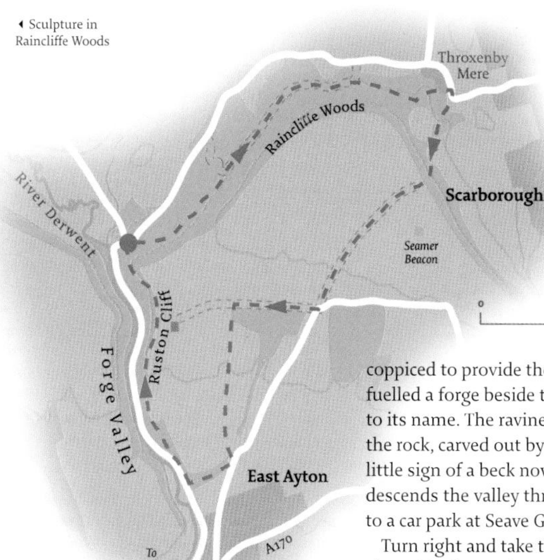

running alongside a wood for just under 1km. Where the wood ends, turn left at its corner and follow a bridleway (no sign) between the wood and the field. Later it becomes a green lane and emerges onto a wider track at the head of a ravine. Don't follow the track to the left or go right into the field; instead, find a footpath to the right (easily missed) on the near side of the ravine, tracing a route between this and the field. You are now entering the Forge Valley National Nature Reserve.

With its complex geology and varied wildlife, this is one of the best examples of a valley-side mixed deciduous wood in England's North East. Trees were once coppiced to provide the charcoal that fuelled a forge beside the river, giving rise to its name. The ravine is a deep cleft in the rock, carved out by water but with little sign of a beck now. A good path descends the valley through beechwoods to a car park at Seave Gate Gill.

Turn right and take the footpath alongside the road, noting the limestone cliffs up on the right through the trees. In 300m, come to a small car park on the right at Wallis's Quarry. Turn into this and follow the footpath rising out of it. Keep climbing the path, ignoring a track to the left. Higher up, bear left at the side of a small trench and follow a path as it curves round and along the top of the woods. It stays inside the woods, with fields over the wall to the right. Now running along the top of Ruston Cliff Wood, it later passes the buildings at Osborne Lodge. Soon afterwards, bear left, keeping to the main path as it passes a seat and begins to rake downhill. Pass a disused quarry and then continue to descend steeply. A final section of path leads to the car park at Green Gate.

The Hole of Horcum

Distance 9km Time 3 hours
Terrain moorland paths and tracks
Map OS Explorer OL 27 Access Coastliner bus (840) from Leeds, York and Whitby to the A169 car park

The road from Pickering to Whitby gradually climbs to the moors, reaching its climax as it passes the Hole of Horcum and crosses the narrow isthmus above Saltergate. North of here, the moors stretch beyond Fylingdales towards the sea at Whitby. The Hole of Horcum is a deep moorland bowl, into which a number of small valleys or 'griffs' combine to form the headwaters of Levisham Beck. Of course, its real origin lies in a domestic squabble. Sometime in the mists of prehistory, a giant scooped out a handful of earth to throw at his wife, leaving the great cauldron behind.

From the viewpoint at Hole of Horcum, the walk plunges into the bowl itself. It explores the ravine of Dundale Griff before returning on an ancient moorland track. You can combine this with the next walk to make a longer figure of eight, with the crossover at Dundale Pond.

There is a large car park (charge) on the A169, around 11km north of Pickering. The regular Coastliner bus also stops here. Cross the very fast and busy A169. Go down a few steps opposite and turn right to follow a footpath just below and parallel to the road. This follows the line of Horcum Dike. After about 500m, you come to the nape of the ridge. The main road is above to the right, making a sharp hairpin that drops down to Saltergate. At a junction of paths, bear left to take the path down into the Hole of Horcum. The noise of the A169 soon disperses

and the route descends steadily between heather and bracken into the cauldron itself. An excellent hardcore path crosses open heath and, at the bottom, goes through a gate. Continue on a broad grass path, tracing the side of the valley of the Levisham Beck as it drives a route out of the Hole of Horcum. Pass the derelict building at Low Horcum, part-renovated in 2011 – not for humans but for bats and other wildlife. In a small grassy side valley, keep right at a fork, following the main valley just above the beck and below woodland. It crosses a couple of curious mounds, the remains of Cross Dyke, an old boundary marker. You eventually come to a gate, leading to an area of undergrowth and small trees. Duckboards help the way through here and a narrow path continues through the bracken. Shortly after a footbridge, you come to a junction of paths.

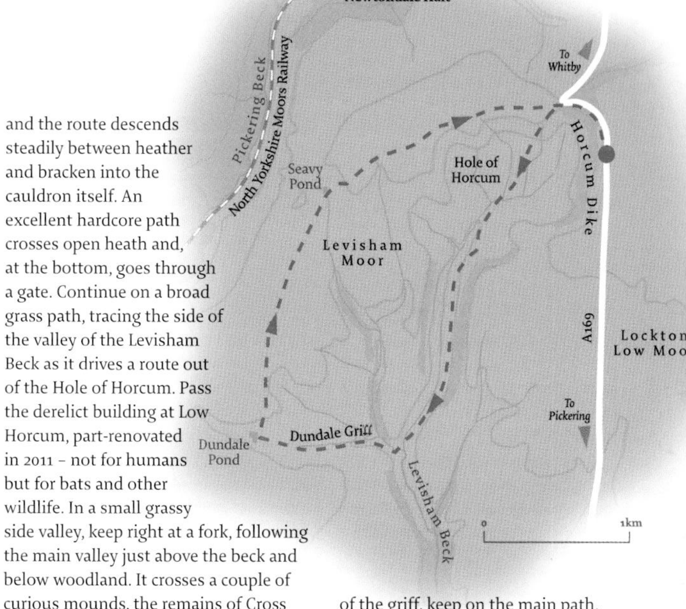

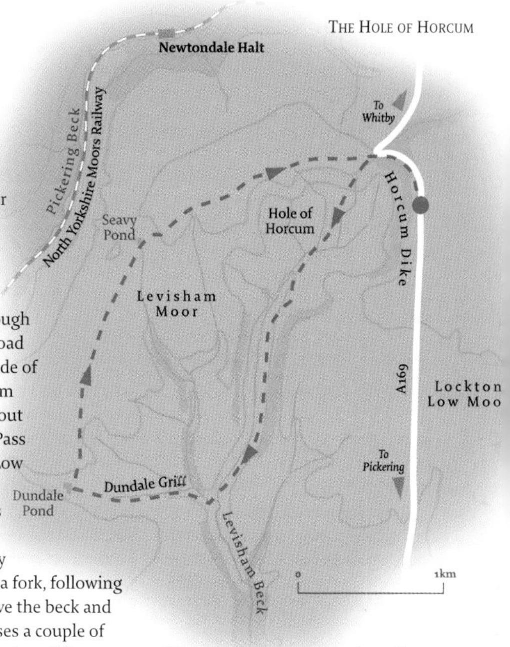

Turn right, now following Dundale Griff, a narrow steep-sided ravine, originally scoured by torrents of water running off the moors. The path cleaves to the side of the ravine. Oak, rowan and silver birch trees cling to its vertiginous sides, while heather, bracken and bilberries cover the hills above. At the top of the griff, keep on the main path, trending right, crossing some open reedy land and aiming for a fingerpost on the horizon. Five routes meet here at Dundale Pond. A stone records how the land was given to the monks of Malton Priory in about 1230 as pasture for their sheep.

Turn right here, taking the path signed to Saltergate. A short climb brings you onto the moorland plateau, and a good wide track rises gently ahead. It's around 2.5km back to the main road. About halfway along, pass Seavy Pond, before veering round to the right above the Hole of Horcum. Return on the path below the road and back to the car park.

◂ To the Hole of Horcum

Levisham and Newton Dale

Distance **10km** Time **2 hours 30**
Terrain **tracks, woodland paths; careful navigation needed** Map **OS Explorer OL 27**
Access **no regular public transport, apart from steam trains on the North Yorkshire Moors Railway**

A great exploration of the wooded valleys of Newton Dale and Levisham Beck. You can combine this with the previous walk to make a longer figure-of-eight route that takes in the Hole of Horcum. The crossover is at Dundale Pond.

Start from the Horseshoe Inn at the top end of Levisham village; there is limited parking in the village. Take Limpsey Gate Lane, which goes to the right-hand side of the pub as you face the front, climbing gradually towards Levisham Moor. The lane becomes a track and then ends at a gate. Continue on a grassy track across the moor for about 300m before coming to a junction of paths next to Dundale Pond.

Turn left, following the sign to Levisham Station with the pond on your right. A path follows the course of a shallow valley. In 500m, at a wall corner, keep straight ahead with the wall on your left. Where the wall later turns sharply to the left, carry straight on across rough grassland to reach an abrupt edge, with the ground falling steeply ahead to the deep cleft of Newton Dale. Bear right to find a path that rakes down the side of the bank, heading through bracken to reach a level path at the bottom.

Turn left at the signpost. In 400m, the path reaches a road on an elbow junction. Turn right here and follow the road down into the wooded depths of Newton Dale to a level crossing at Levisham Station. Steam trains between Whitby and Pickering call here.

Beyond the level crossing, continue on the forestry road that travels along the floor of the valley. In about 500m, soon

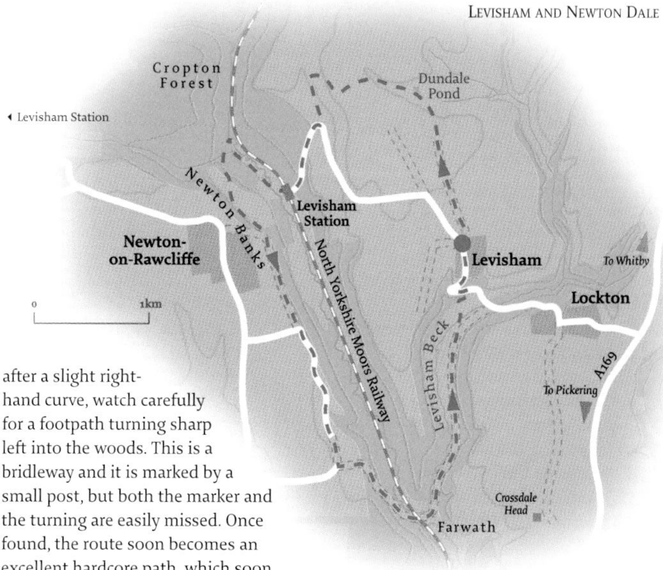

after a slight right-hand curve, watch carefully for a footpath turning sharp left into the woods. This is a bridleway and it is marked by a small post, but both the marker and the turning are easily missed. Once found, the route soon becomes an excellent hardcore path, which soon slants up the side of Newton Banks through a blend of woodland and clearings. At the top, turn left; take the level track along the edge of the bank, which is also the route of the Tabular Hills Walk. The village of Newton-on-Rawcliffe is just a field away on the right, though little of it is visible. Follow the track and then rough road for nearly 2km until you come to a T-junction.

Turn left. The broad track soon veers right, descending the bank diagonally. At the bottom, a footbridge crosses the beck at Farwath. Continue over a level crossing and pass through the farmyard. Keep straight ahead to a gate. Beyond this, ignore the track to the right and carry straight on, trending left. Another gate leads onto a woodland track, Sleights Road. Follow this for about 1.25km through woods and fields.

Look out for an old church down in the valley to the left. This is the redundant parish church of Levisham, closed in the 1950s. Just after a gate, a footpath bears left off the main track and descends into the valley. It crosses a footbridge, then goes up to the right of the church. At the top of the field above the church, turn right onto a track, which soon comes to a road. Turn left, climbing uphill for a short distance. Watch out for a footpath turning uphill sharply to the right with a sign for the Tabular Hills Walk. Climb this steeply, turning left at a junction to reach Levisham village.

The Bridestones

Distance 4km **Time** 1 hour
Terrain woodland paths, rocky and steep in places **Map** OS Explorer OL 27
Access no regular bus service; check moorsbus.org to find out about any summer Sunday or Bank Holiday services

Dalby Forest has more than 3000 hectares of woodland with a wide range of waymarked trails for walking and cycling. There is an 11km toll road through the heart of the forest which gives access to several car parks and other attractions. Just outside the fringe of Dalby Forest, the Bridestones are curious weathered sandstone outcrops separated by a deep trench in a nature reserve comprising heather moor and birdlife-rich woodland. The walk approaches High Bridestones through a wooded valley, circles around the head of the griff to reach Low Bridestones and then descends back through the woodland.

To reach the Dalby Forest toll road, take a side turning 2km or so north of Thornton-le-Dale and follow this down to the forest toll. Alternatively, from the Scarborough side, use minor roads through Hackness and Langdale End. There is a visitor centre, café, cycle hire and rope activity centre in the heart of the forest. Of course, not all of these are included in the toll!

The walk starts at Bridestones car park, which is about 3km beyond the visitor centre if you're driving east. Take the hardcore path which leads from the back of the car park.

A short walk brings you to National Trust land at the beginning of Bridestones Moor Nature Reserve. Where the path turns right, up into woodland, keep straight ahead through a kissing gate, below the wood and across the top of fields. Oak and pine trees cling

to the steep sides to the right, while open meadows cover the valley floor.

Just before you come to some stepping stones over a small beck, turn right to go through a kissing gate into the Bridestones Moor Nature Reserve. Cross the beck on a footbridge, entering Dove Dale. The path weaves through the long grass in the clearing, then meanders along the valley. After another footbridge, it begins to climb up towards High Bridestones on a steep stone pathway, gaining a ridge of land, known as Needle Point. As you climb, look across to Low Bridestones on the skyline across the trench of Bridestone Griff. The path levels out onto a plateau of heather and bracken, reaching High Bridestones. There is a junction by the first stone and the route turns right here. (First, you could wander along the path ahead to explore some of the other outcrops.) The path dips down across the heather-clad Bridestone Griff and continues on up the other side to pass Low Bridestones on a level path. Keep straight ahead at the last stone outcrop. Soon the path begins to descend, turning left through larch and birch trees back to the start.

If you want a further saunter, there is a waymarked circuit of Staindale Lake, just a short way up the road past the toilets, or find a link on the other side of the road from Bridestones car park.

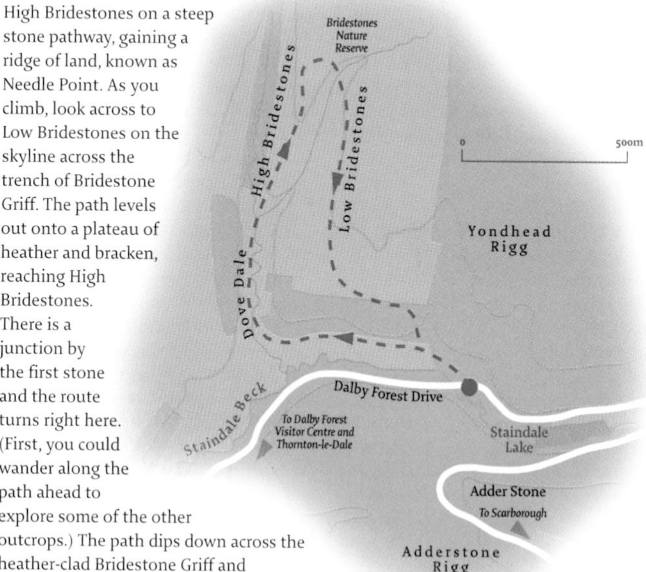

◂ The Bridestones

Crosscliff View Trail to Jerry Noddle

Distance 5km Time 1 hour 30
Terrain level forest roads and tracks
Map OS Explorer OL 27 Access no regular bus service; check moorsbus.org to find out about any summer Sunday or Bank Holiday services

Dalby Forest is an extensive area of woodland in the southeastern part of the North York Moors National Park. The forest plateau is segmented by many steep-sided valleys, alternating with wooded 'riggs', or ridges. This is an easy circuit around the edge of the plateau, offering great viewpoints at Crosscliff and Jerry Noddle.

There is an 11km toll road through the heart of the forest which gives access to a number of car parks and other attractions. To reach the toll road, take a side turning about 2km north of Thornton-le-Dale and follow this down to the forest toll. Alternatively, from the Scarborough side, use minor roads through Hackness and Langdale End.

Start from Cross Cliff car park. This is signposted off the Dalby Forest toll road, about 6km after the visitor centre if you're driving east. A forest road leads to the main (not disabled) car park in about 1km. Find the pull-in by the sign for the start of the Crosscliff View Trail.

Follow the path into the forest past a number of ditches. These are part of Dargate Dikes which probably date from the Bronze Age. They may have been boundary markers or used in connection with farming. In about 300m, you suddenly arrive at the top of the escarpment at Cross Cliff viewpoint. The land falls away abruptly in front of you into the valley of Crosscliff Beck. The forest stretches into the distance, with Fylingdales Early Warning Station in the distance. Turn right to soon come to a junction of tracks at the disabled car park.

◂ Track on Jerry Noddle

Continue straight ahead on the forest road as it runs along the edge of the escarpment, with views to the north.

In 1.5km, the wedge of land reaches a point, like the stern of a ship, known as Jerry Noddle. Wooded valleys extend down ahead. Their waters feed the Derwent which, although tantalisingly close to the sea at Scarborough, turns a great wheel southwestwards through York, eventually mixing with saltwater in the Humber Estuary.

Follow the track as it turns sharply right. In a while, it bends right again around Rigg Noddle towards the cleft of Great Gill. Cleared areas afford extensive views across the forest. Keep on the main track as it weaves around the top of Great Gill, ignoring any left and right turns, until you reach a T-junction at Fox How, a small Bronze Age burial mound on the left of the path, next to a solitary oak tree.

Turn right. This is the access track for the car park. In 1km, at a junction, bear left to reach the start of the walk, or right to reach the disabled car park.

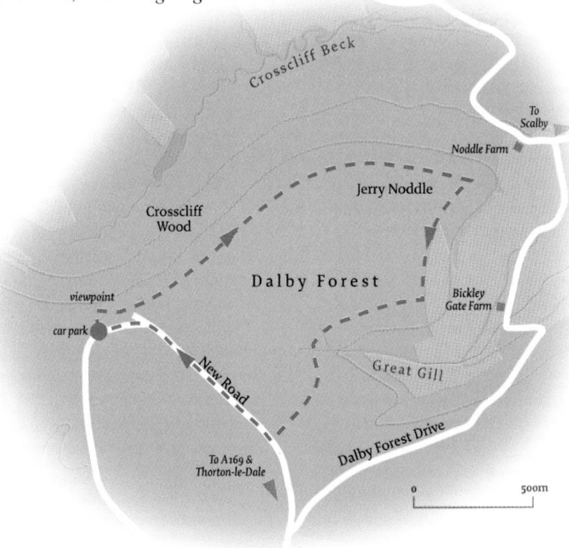

Whisper Dales and Broxa Forest

Distance 7km Time 2 hours 30
Terrain forest tracks and lanes. Some stretches of footpath may be overgrown in high summer Map OS Explorer OL 27
Access no regular public transport to the start

A series of little dales claws into the ridge of Broxa Forest, with small becks emerging from the woods where they are spawned, dropping through these tranquil valleys to coalesce into the River Derwent. In old language the river is named after the oak tree, and Broxa Forest has a wide range of mixed woodland as well as inevitable conifer plantations. The walk begins on Reasty Hill Top, dropping into the haven of Whisper Dales before returning to the forest through neighbouring High Dales.

Start at the car park at Reasty Hill Top, near Harwood Dale. Cross the road and follow the track next to a large sign for North Riding Forest Park. Follow this for a short distance until you come to a junction and then turn left along a broad, level avenue. In 500m the track bends to the left and drops steeply towards Whisper Dales. As it approaches the valley, the track leaves the forest and soon afterwards it curves right into the grounds of Whisperdales. However, the bridleway bypasses the house and continues along grassy meadows at the bottom of this lovely secluded valley, with the forest climbing the hillsides above.

Keep straight ahead along this rough track for about 2km, later crossing the beck and ignoring any side turnings. Eventually it merges into a lane by a group of houses. Negotiate two fords, using the adjacent footbridges. After the last house, you reach a road junction and turn right.

A narrow, shaded lane winds gradually uphill for about 1km, at first next to a

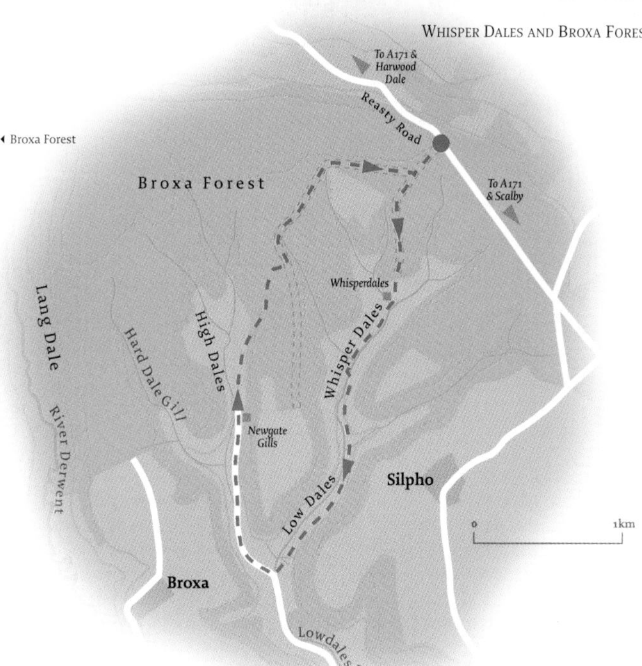

small beck and later marshalled by high hedge banks. Further up, as you approach High Dales, the vista opens out. Where the road ends, keep straight on past the house at Newgate Gills. Immediately after the house, leave the track to take a bridleway climbing diagonally to the right. The first section may suffer from undergrowth, but it soon morphs into a good clear path in pleasant woodland. Continue to rise steadily for almost 1km before reaching a level plateau and clearing. Ignore a turning to the left and instead keep straight ahead.

The track is now wider; it bends to the right and comes to a T-junction. Turn left along this forest road. The route passes along a broad clearing, soon swinging back to the right through a conifer plantation. It's an attractive ride, bordered by heather with conifers complemented by mixed woodland. Ignore any side turnings and keep to the main track when it takes a 90-degree turn to the right, avoiding a faint track straight on. Continue on the track until you come to a T-junction just past a barrier. Turn left to return to the start of the walk.

Through Thornton Dale to Dalby

Distance 17km Time 5 hours Terrain forest tracks, mostly gentle gradients Map OS Explorer OL 27 Access Coastliner bus (841) from Leeds, York and Whitby to Thornton-le-Dale

A rewarding expedition from the lovely village of Thornton-le-Dale into Dalby Forest. An alternative start would be at Dalby Forest Visitor Centre, making the walk just a circuit of the forest, although this would incur the road toll and also miss out the picturesque approach.

Start from the crossroads in the centre of Thornton-le-Dale. Walk alongside the A170 Scarborough road for about 200m, past the row of almshouses built in 1670 to accommodate some of the parish's poor, then turn left up Brook Lane. (If you continue just along the main road to the bridge over Thornton Beck, you'll see the much photographed Beck Isle Cottage in its idyllic riverside situation on the left.)

After about 100m, where Brook Lane bends left, bear right up a lane. This becomes a private road and public footpath. At the end, go through a gate and turn right onto Ellerburn Road, a quiet, wooded lane which leads into the valley of Thornton Beck. There are lots of wayside seats along here.

About 1.5km from Thornton, come to the small hamlet of Ellerburn, passing the 11th-century St Hilda's Church. There is a teashop on the left and a campsite on the right. Keep ahead along the lane. At the far side of the campsite, the lane veers right and then back to the left, past a fish hatchery. It continues as a track along Thornton Dale, the tranquil beck lined with alder trees. The way draws ever closer to the forest and, about 1km after High Paper Mill Farm, a path and broad forest road lead into Dalby Forest.

Keep straight ahead, ignoring all side turnings. A sequence of small dales drifts up to the right, labelled by the forest authorities and open to walkers and